Classroom Activities for the Busy Teacher: NXT

2nd Edition

Classroom Activities for the Busy Teacher: NXT

Copyright © 2011 by Damien Kee

ISBN – 978-1467920360

About the Author

Dr Damien Kee holds a PhD in Robotics and a Bachelor of Electrical Engineering, both from the University of Queensland, Australia. During his time at the University of Queensland, Damien was the team leader of the Humanoid Robot project that travelled to Japan to compete in RoboCup (2002), as well as the co-team leader of the Mechanical Engineering Student Robotic team that also travelled twice to Japan to compete in RoboCon (1999, 2000). He has built a wide variety of robots, from maze solving mice to humanoids, to robots that could dispense traffic cones.

Damien has been heavily involved with the RoboCup Junior competition since 2001, initially as a judge, and more recently as one of the QLD State competition technical organisers. In 2007, Damien was the Chair of the Organising Committee for the 2007 RoboCup Junior Australian Open that ran successfully with over 140 teams from 3 countries. He has been Chairman of the RoboCup Junior Australian Committee and is the Australian representative to the RoboCup Junior International Committee.

Damien is a member of the LEGO® MINDSTORMS® Community Program, a group of approximately 50 people around the world who consult with LEGO® to make the MINDSTORMS® system a better product. He is also editor-in-chief of the highly popular theNXTstep Blog (www.thenxtstep.com), the leading website for LEGO® MINDSTORMS® users.

Table of Contents

Chapter 1:

Introduction

This book is a guide for teachers implementing a robotics unit in the classroom. It is aimed at middle years schooling (ages 9 - 15) but the wide range of activities can be adapted to suit older or younger students. The book is based around a single robot, the DomaBot, which is used in all activities. This approach is valuable in resource limited classrooms, as it allows the teacher to work with a 'standard' robot, rather than using valuable classroom time building and breaking down robots each lesson.

It is assumed that the teacher has a basic knowledge of how to open the NXT-G programming environment and how to download a program to the NXT unit.

The book is divided into sections that follow a 10 week plan, although this can be modified to suit the needs of the teacher. The first 4 weeks takes students through a series of activities, progressively exposing them to new aspects of the NXT-G programming environment. Following that, is a set of open ended challenges from which teachers may pick and choose to suit their particular class.

All challenges include the following information:

- Scenario setup + background information. Teachers are free to develop each scenario further as they see fit.
- Equipment list. Aside from the standard NXT robotics kit, all other required resources are easily sourced within a school environment.
- Teacher notes are provided on common issues that may arise with each challenge and how they are best dealt with.
- Programming examples in the NXT-G development environment.
- Student worksheets to fill out (photocopy permission provided).
- Extension activities.

Lesson Plan

The following is a lesson structure for a 10 week unit on robotics. This plan assumes approximately 5 hours of content per week in class, although the ability of the students involved may require slightly more or less time as needed.

Week 1: Introduction

Students are introduced to robotics in general. Their use in society and the differences between fictional and real robots are described and the fundamental components of a robot are discussed. Students are asked to prepare a report on robots. Student worksheet – What is a Robot? is handed out with the due date left to the teacher's discretion.

Week 2: Organisation

NXT kits are sorted to ensure all pieces are accounted for. The concept of flowcharting is presented, and backed up by worksheet - Flowcharting. During this week students will also build the DomaBot or another equivalent robot. Students can continue to work on the previous week's assignment.

Week 3: DomaBot Basics

Students will learn how to use the NXT-G programming language to move their robot around the floor using Student worksheet – DomaBot Basics. The 'Move' block is the focal point of this week's challenge.

Week 4: How Far, How Fast: Data collection

Following on from the previous week, students will use their robots to learn about velocity and data collection.

Week 5: How Many Sides?

The drawing attachment is constructed and mounted onto the robot. Students will learn about the 'loop' structure as well as building on their knowledge of geometric shapes. Polygon properties such as internal and external angles are discussed.

Week 6: Help! I'm Stuck! + Help! I'm Still Stuck

The concepts of sensors are introduced and the Touch Sensor and Ultrasonic Sensors are used to assist the robot with navigation. Students give their robot the intelligence necessary to make decisions for itself.

Week 7 Stay Away from the Edge + Did you Hear that?

Additional sensors are presented to round out the full complement of standard NXT sensors available. The Light Sensor and Sound Sensor are connected and provide additional sources of information to the robot.

Week 8: Major Project (Mini- Golf, Dancing Robots, Robot Wave or Robot Butler)

Teachers may choose one or a number of these activities for the students to undertake. They may work in small or large teams, each with a few robots per team. Student may wish to pursue their own project, in consultation with the teacher.

Week 9: Major Project

Students continue working on their major project.

Week 10: As Seen on TV!

Students develop a multimedia marketing presentation with which to 'sell' their robot to consumers. This may take on any number of media formats (website, speech, newsletter article etc.)

Resources

Extra resources that complement this book can be found on the website

http://www.damienkee.com

Chapter 2:

What is a robot?

Overview: Discover what a robot is, and what function it performs.

Project: Students are asked about what they think a robot is, and what it does. Students research robots in general and present a report based on one particular robot.

Equipment

- Access to research materials, (Library, Internet etc)
- Computer to write report

Teachers Notes

This section will cover the following concepts

- Research skills
- Report writing
- Word Processing
- Design with Multimedia
- Oral presentation

Photocopy Student Handout 1 and distribute to the class. You may choose to start discussion immediately or give the students time to perform preliminary research. Bring the group together and start to form a class opinion of robots.

Answer the following questions as a group.

- What is a robot?
- Where did the term 'robot' come from?
- Name some types of robots
- Why do we have robots / What function do they perform in society?
- What are the main components of a robot?

There are many different interpretations of what a robot is, with some of them quite different. There is no single definitive answer that encapsulates all the functions of a robot. The following is a list of different dictionary definitions available.

American Heritage Dictionary

"A mechanical device that sometimes resembles a human and is capable of performing a variety of often complex human tasks on command or by being programmed in advance.

A machine or device that operates automatically or by remote control"

Cambridge Advanced Learner's Dictionary

"a machine used to perform jobs automatically, which is controlled by a computer"

Oxford Dictionary

"a machine capable of carrying out a complex series of actions automatically, especially one programmable by a computer."

Keep in mind that while there is no universally accepted definition of a robot, the following points seem to cover the vast majority of robots.

- A robot is artificial. It has been manufactured and does not occur naturally.
- It is controlled by a computer of some description. This may range from a full sized personal computer to a small embedded micro-controller.
- It can sense the surrounding environment
- It can perform actions movements

Despite these requirements, it is still very difficult to categorise a robot. The question can be posed to students; Is a washing machine a robot?

- It is artificial
- Modern washing machines are controlled by miniature computers inside them.
- They can sense when the lid is open.
- They perform movements by spinning the clothes back and forth.

Could railway boom gates be consider a robot?

- They are artificial
- They are controlled by computers
- They can sense when a train is approaching
- They can raise and lower the boom gates

Why do we have Robots?

There are many reasons that robots are used in society, each one filling a particular need. This question may also be posed as:

"What advantages are achieved by having robots in certain situations?"

Robots are generally built to serve for what is commonly known as the 3 D's; Dull, Dirty and Dangerous.

In an industrial setting, the use of robots allows repetitive tasks to be performed accurately time after time. Robots can generally perform simple task far quicker than humans can. This leads to increased productivity and better quality control of goods. Some types of robots, particularly those that need to pick up and put down fragile items, are so accurate that they can stop within a human hairs width of the objects they need to manipulate. Medical robots are reaping the benefits of such accuracy, allowing doctors to perform surgery on patients who are in another city or on the other side of the world.

Exploratory robots and military robots are designed to keep people away from harmful situations. Robot operators can drive a robot into an unsafe area, and use the sensors and cameras on board to gather information. This is particularly useful for search and rescue missions in disaster areas, where the environment may be unsafe for humans to go looking for survivors.

Entertainment robots provide a lot of fun and interest for people. They can be typically found on TV, highlighting the fun things that robots can do. The range of sophistication goes from the very complex humanoids such as ASIMO and QRIO, to the toys like RoboSapien and the LEGO® NXT system. Household robots such as the vacuuming Roomba was one of the first robots to be marketed as a domestic robot. Later versions have been developed that will also mop our floors and clean our gutters. The dream of a robotic butler to pick up our clothes and do our chores is not far away.

Name different types of robots?

There are a variety of different categories for robots, including but not limited to:

- Entertainment (ASIMO, QRIO, AiBO, animatronics, RoboSapien, LEGO®)
- Domestic (Roomba, automatic lawn mowers)
- Movies (C3PO, R2D2, Terminator, Johnny 5)
- Industrial (welding, Pick and Place, factory automation)
- Medical (remote surgery, minimally invasive surgery)
- Exploratory (Mars rovers, deep sea ROV's, unassisted aerial vehicles)
- Military (PackBot, bomb disposal, search and rescue)

What are the main components of a robot?

Robots can be broken down into three distinct components; sensors, computation and actuators.

Sensors are used to 'feel' the surrounding environment. The robot uses these sensors to take in information about where it is and what it is doing. Different sensors can be used to sense different conditions including light and dark, temperature, bump sensors, ultrasonic, infrared... the list goes on and on. Think about what sensors a human has, and how a robot replicates them. Sensors are classed as inputs, that is, they take information and input it into the robot's brain.

The computation component consists of an onboard computer that the robot uses to process the information coming from its sensors. This can be as small as a few computer chips right through to a full personal computer. The level of complexity of the required tasks will dictate the amount of computational ability needed by the robot.

The last distinct component of a robot is its actuators. Actuators are a fancy way of saying 'bits that move'. These may be motors in the wheels, or engines that make the arms go back and forth. It could also be hydraulic pistons or pneumatic cylinders. Actuators are a form of outputs, along with lights and speakers. The robot brain tells these outputs to do different tasks.

Generally speaking, the sensors provide the information to the computers, which in turn tell the motors what to do.

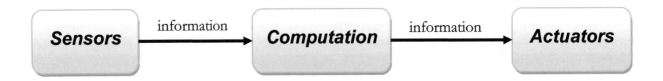

Path of information flow in a robot

Where did the term 'Robot' come from?

While the idea of artificial beings have been around for many years, the term 'robot' was first coined by Czech writer Karel Čapek in his play R.U.R. (Rossum's Universal Robots) in 1920. The word is derived from the Czech 'robota', which translates as 'forced work', 'slave' or 'servitude'. Čapek credits his brother Josef as the true inventor of the word.

Robots have enjoyed the majority of their exposure through movies and science fiction writings, such Star Wars and the Asimov series of 'Robot' books.

Robots in their presently accepted state were first developed in the 1950's, with George Devol's Unimate robot, capable of lifting hot pieces of metal from a die casting machine and stacking them. The first Unimate was sold to a General Motors assembly plant in New Jersey.

Assessment

Students are to present a report on robots. This may be done as a report, PowerPoint presentation, poster or oral report. Students will give a brief overview of robotics based on the preceding discussion and perform a more in depth analysis of one particular robot as approved by the teacher.

The following is a good list of real world robots.

- ASIMO, QRIO, AIBO, Roomba
- Spirit / Opportunity
- Pathfinder Sojourner
- PUMA arm, SCARA arm

Decide on the format of the assignment (written, oral, multimedia) and hand out the Student Worksheet – What is a Robot?. The due date is left to the teacher discretion.

Extension activities

Any of the following questions could be used to promote further discussion:

- What are the differences between real robots and fictional robots?
- What attributes of robots are still only being dreamed about?
- Should robots have rights?
- Does a robot have a right to be cared for and maintained?
- Is there such a concept as robot abuse?

Watch the movie or read the book 'Bicentennial Man'

- Should a robot be compensated for its work?
- What form should payment entail? Monetary? Upgrades?

Watch the movie or read the book 'I, Robot'

- Can robots be charged with a crime?
- If someone is injured by a robot, is it a crime or a malfunction?
- Will robots make some jobs redundant?

Robots are replacing many people who work in dull, dirty or dangerous jobs.

- Will robots working in dull jobs force people to learn more complex skill sets?
- Will the proliferation of robots result in more robot maintenance jobs?
- What other new technologies have threatened jobs in the past? Industrial revolution etc.

Look into the RoboCup mission for 2050

> *"By the year 2050, develop a team of fully autonomous humanoid robots that can win against the human world soccer champion group."*

Chapter 3:

Flowcharting

Overview: An introduction to flowcharting

Project: Students are introduced to the concept of flowcharting. This process will allow them to co-ordinate their thoughts and will make programming less difficult as they progress. A larger project is systematically broken down into a series of more manageable tasks that are more readily completed.

Equipment

- Blackboard / Whiteboard
- Markers

Teachers Notes

This section will cover the following concepts

- Flowcharting / storyboarding
- Progression of actions

This section is best done on a whiteboard or blackboard. The concept of a flowchart should be explained with emphasis on both the correct order of tasks and providing sufficient detail. With both these concepts understood, generating a program for a robot becomes considerably easier.

Theory

When planning the program for a robot, it is very beneficial to go through a flow charting process. Flow charting allows us to take the ideas we have for a robot, and start to assemble them in a logical fashion.

As an example, let us have a look at a typical student morning. We will look at how we approach our morning as a series of different individual tasks. First up, we need to get the order in which we do each step the right way around. If we try and do things in the wrong order, the whole day may not work. In addition, the amount of detail for each task is important. Each step should be sufficiently small enough, so as it can be done as a single step. If we keep these tasks short and simple and concise, it is easier plan out the bigger tasks. Occasionally, some steps need to be revisited and broken down further into smaller steps.

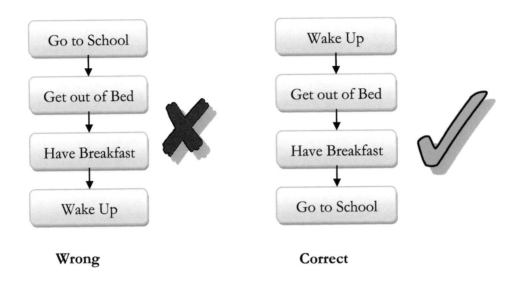

Wrong   **Correct**

The order in which we do each task is very important. If we get the order around the wrong way, the tasks will not make sense.

When we start programming our robots, we will also need to sketch out a flowchart of how we would like our robot to behave. If we can break down the whole program into little tasks like we did above, it will be easier to program our robot. Ideally, each individual task will relate directly to a single block in the NXT-G programming environment. Once we have this sequence of tasks, we can start putting them into a language that the robot will understand. We will be using the NXT-G programming language to make our robot perform each of these tasks that we have defined.

It is important to remember that the first draft is not expected to be perfect. Changes will almost certainly have to be made along the way as flaws and inconsistencies are found. It will need to be stressed that it is vital to have a plan or road map first, before we start programming, even if that plan changes along the way.

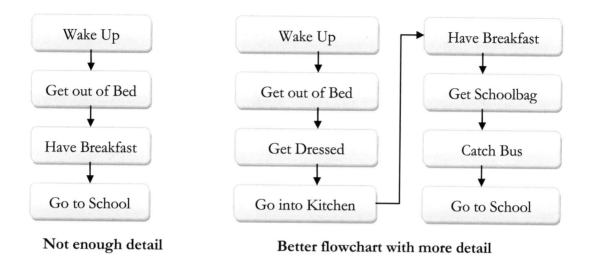

Not enough detail　　　　**Better flowchart with more detail**

How much detail we put into our flowchart is important. The one on the left has only a few broad steps. The one on the right is far more detailed and would be easier to convert into a program.

Assessment

Photocopy and hand out Student Worksheet - Flowcharting. Lead the class in a discussion about flowcharting and have the students complete the worksheet. Emphasise the need to have the correct order of tasks as well as sufficient detail.

Chapter 4:

DomaBot Basics

Overview: Build a robot that is capable of driving around an obstacle course.

Project: NASA is in the market for a new planetary rover to explore the recently discover planet NXTopia. You are required to design and construct a robot that is capable of following a set of commands to explore the planet's surface. Before the robot is deployed, it must be extensively tested to ensure it will perform as expected. You can't fly a technician to NXTopia to reboot the robot!

Equipment required

- 1 NXT robot kit per group
- 1 computer per group
- Masking tape
- Tape measure

Teachers Notes

This section will cover the following topics amongst others

- Basic numeracy
- Decimal and fractional numbers
- Relationship between diameter and circumference
- Conversion between millimetres and inches

Get the students to build DomaBot robot presented in Building Instructions.

Photocopy and hand out Student Worksheet – DomaBot Basics. This worksheet gives the students a range of different activities to follow that progressively increase in difficulty.

NXT-G Specific

To perform the programming, we will need to know about the **Move** block from the common palette. The **Move** block as its name implies, controls the movement of up to 3 motors. The diagram below shows the **Move** block and its associated properties.

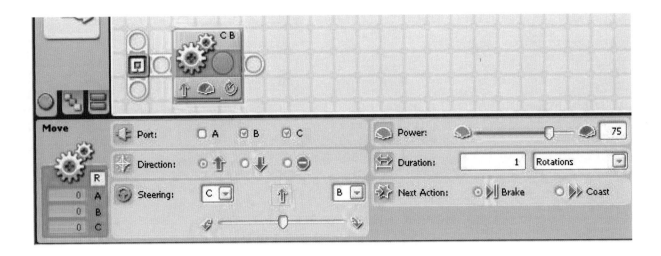

Port: This selects which port the motor is connected to. The default is ports B and C which is identical to the DomaBot design.

Direction: Is the motor going in a generally forward direction or generally backward direction or is it stopped altogether?

Steering: The steering angle is controlled via the slider bar at the bottom of the configuration panel. This will range from a gentle turn to a tight turn on the spot depending on how far this slider is taken. For a student's perspective have a look at a bicycle. If we turn the handle bars a little, we get a gentle curve. The sharper we turn the handle bars, the smaller the turning circle we will get.

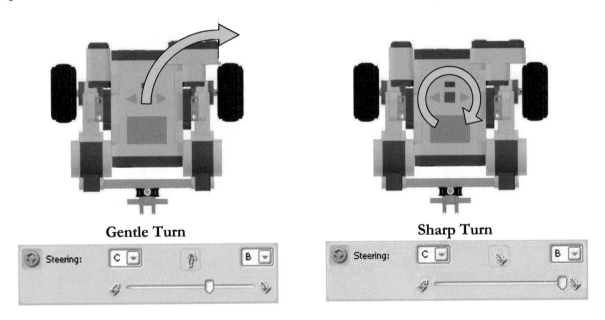

The slider itself however does not control how far the robot travels. Take the analogy of the car. We can turn the steering wheel all we want, but if we don't put our foot on the accelerator, then the car will not move at all. The distance travelled by the car (either in a straight line or in a curve) is determined by the 'duration' that the accelerator is held down for.

Power: This slider controls how fast the motor goes. Be aware that at low speeds the motor may not have enough torque (turning force) to make the robot move. Generally speaking, power levels of 10-100 are appropriate for most robot designs.

Duration: The most important property of the configuration box. This will control how long the motor will turn for. There are 4 options, unlimited, degrees, rotations and seconds. For the first few sections, we will be using just the degrees and rotations options. These refer to how far the wheels of the robot turn.

Next Action: We can specify what we need the motor to do after it has completed its required duration. The two options are brake and coast. The difference between each property is the same as in a real car. If the brakes are applied, the motor come to a sudden stop. If it is allowed to coast, the robot is allowed to slowly come to a stop.

Theory

The first step required is to characterise the robots performance. This means, take measurements to determine the specifications of the robots movement. This is a good opportunity to either reinforce or introduce the correlation between the radius of a wheel and its circumference.

Calculating the circumference can be done either mathematically or experimentally depending on the ability of the students.

Mathematically: The circumference of a wheel can be calculated using the formulae: $c = \pi \times d$

Where c= circumference, π = 3.14 (approx) and d is the diameter of the wheel.

The wheel that comes as part of the standard NXT set is 56mm (2.2 inch) in diameter which results in a circumference of approximately 176mm (6.9 inch).

Experimentally: Take a wheel off the robot and make a mark on the tire with either chalk or masking tape. Create a starting mark on the table and line up our tire mark with it. Now slowly roll the wheel until the tire mark again touches the ground. Make another mark at this point and use a ruler to measure the distance.

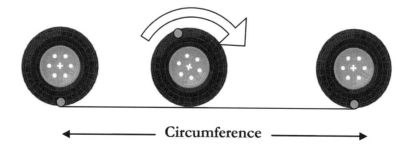

Circumference

For the challenge where students are asked to make their robots turn 180 degrees, they will typically type in 180 degrees and download it. When they come to run the program though, they will find that their robot will not actually turn 180 degrees but in fact, if they are using the DomaBot design, it will only turn 45 degrees.

This behaviour occurs because the move block is designed to control the *wheel* of the robot, not the whole robot. If we observe the wheel, we will find that it does in fact turn exactly 180 degrees, just as it was told to do. The angle turned by the robot however is dependent on a few different conditions such as the size of the wheels and the distance between the wheels. To test, place a strip of tape on the floor. Start the robot with both wheels on the tape. A perfect 180 degree turn will result in the wheels ending up back on the tape.

Calculating the required duration to make the robot turn 180 degrees can be done either mathematically or experimentally depending on the ability of the students.

Mathematically: The robot needs to trace out half a circle that is defined by the distance between the 2 wheels. On the DomaBot, this is 168mm (6.6 inch).

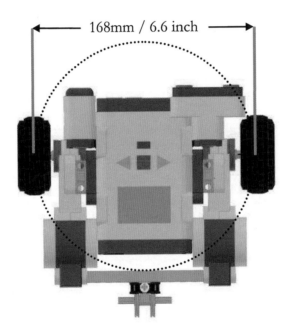

This distance can be calculated as half the circumference of a 168mm (6.6 inch) diameter circle.

$$\text{distance} = \frac{\pi \times 168\text{mm}}{2} = \frac{\pi \times 6.6\text{ inch}}{2}$$

$$\text{distance} = \quad 264\text{mm} \quad = 10.4\text{ inch}$$

We know from the previous exercise that the circumference of the wheel is 176mm (6.9 inch). We know that the wheel must travel 264mm (10.4 inch) to perform a half circle robot rotation so the duration the wheel must turn can be calculated as follows:

$$\text{duration} = \frac{264\text{mm}}{176\text{mm}} = \frac{10.4\text{inch}}{6.9\text{inch}}$$

$$\text{duration} = 1.5 \text{ rotations or } 540 \text{ degrees}$$

Experimentally: Keep increasing the duration parameter until the robot does indeed turn 180 degrees. Students perform trial and error with different values until an acceptable solution is found.

Why is my robot not perfect?

Using the standard DomaBot design, the wheels *should* be located 168mm (6.6 inch) apart. If those wheels happen to slide along the axles shafts, this will make the wheel base slightly larger and will change how many degrees are required to do a full 180 degree robot rotation.

Let us take the example that the wheels are 1mm further out on both sides, giving a total wheel base of 170mm. We now have a required travel distance of:

$$\text{distance} = \frac{\pi \times 170\text{mm}}{2}$$

$$\text{distance} = 267\text{mm}$$

The duration required for the wheels to travel 267mm is:

$$\text{duration} = \frac{267}{176}$$

$$\text{duration} = 1.52 \text{ rotations or } 546 \text{ degrees}$$

Larger spacing of the wheels will result in a larger required duration.

Look out for...

Layout two strips of tape, 500mm apart as our test distance. The 180 degree turn may introduce a slight offset, requiring a little more duration on the 3rd block to drive back to the starting point.

The duration required to go 500mm (OR 20 inch) can be calculated by dividing 500mm by the circumference of the wheel (176mm / 6.9 inch).

$$x = \frac{500}{176} \qquad \text{OR} \qquad \frac{20}{6.9}$$

$$x = 2.84 \text{ rotations OR} \qquad 2.90 \text{ rotations}$$

When running the 'figure of eight' challenge, we can leave it open ended or can specify the shape we require. Encourage the students to draw a picture of the path they are attempting before they start programming. Encourage them to look at each of the individual movements, and relate them back to separate **Move** blocks. To create a test environment, place 2 markers down, 500mm (20 inch) apart. The robots will need to perform their runs around these markers and are not allowed to hit or move the markers. Robots should ideally make it back to where they start.

Here are a variety of different ways of tracing out a 'figure 8'. The digital figure of 8 is the easiest to implement, as the students already know how to drive straight and perform 90 degree turns.

Example Programs

Drive Forward for 90° of the wheels

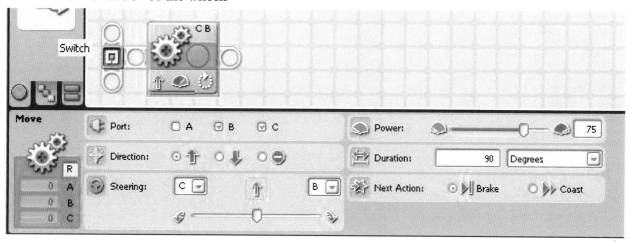

Drive Forward for 0.25 rotations of the wheels

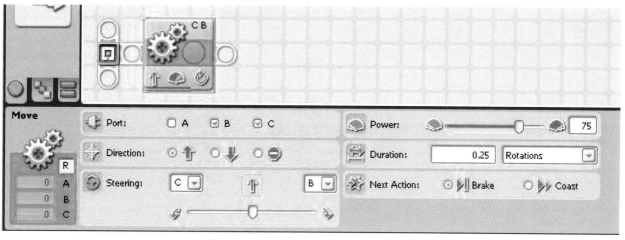

Program your robot to move 3 rotations and measure how far it goes.

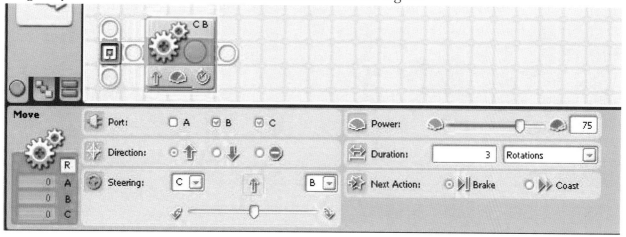

Drive Forward 540° slow, then 540° back as fast as possible

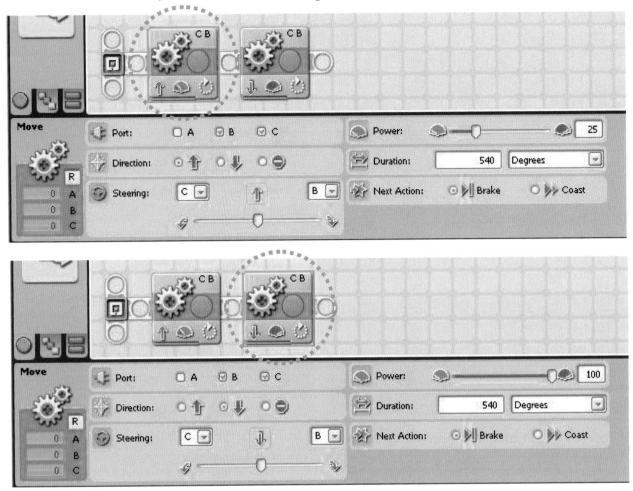

Turn the robot around 180° (The WHEEL needs 540 degrees for the ROBOT to turn 180 degrees)

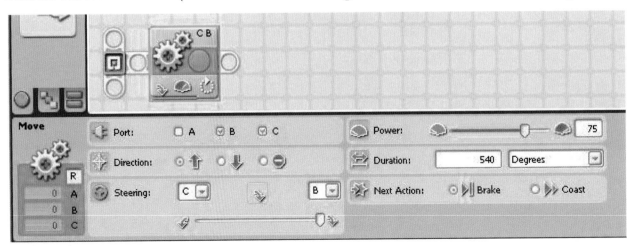

Drive forward for 500mm, turn around 180° and drive back to where you started

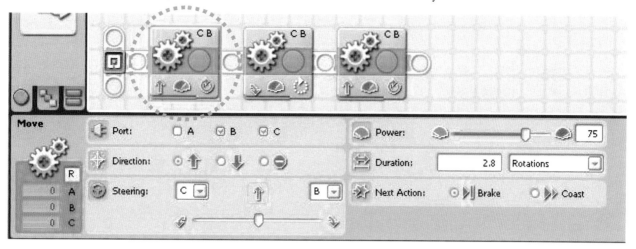

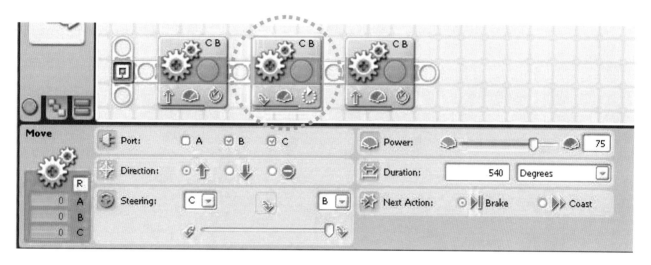

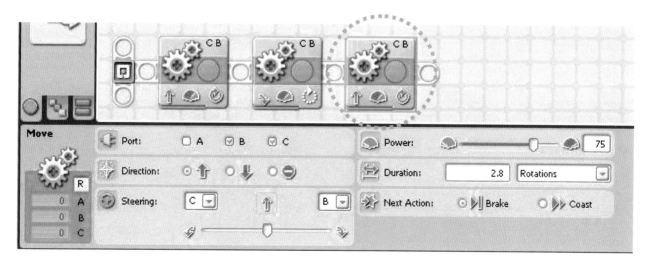

Chapter 5:

How far?

Overview: Test the robot for distance characteristics

Project: In the initial construction of the robot the travelling characteristics are required. After characterising the properties, NASA have asked that you use your data to make predictions about the distance your robot will travel given specific time constraints.

Equipment required

- 1 NXT robot kit per group
- 1 computer per group
- Masking tape
- Tape measure
- Stopwatch

Teachers Notes

This section does not require any additional software knowledge. All activities can be performed with the use of just the **Move** block. The DomaBot is used to perform data gathering and scientific analysis.

Photocopy and hand out Student Worksheet – How Far?.

This section will cover the following topics

- Data gathering
- Graphing
- Interpolation / Extrapolation
- Decimal numbers and fractions
- Averaging of data
- Position and distance

Theory

This activity will look at the effect changing the time of travel of the robot has on the distance it moves. It will become evident that the longer a robot travels, the further it travels but can the relationship between time and distance be predicted?

Students will program their robot to travel for 1 second at a specific power level. The same experiment is run again this time for 2 seconds at the same power level. Students should take as many measurements as time allows with a wide variety of times. Encourage the students to take multiple runs and take the average of all their data to reduce the impact of any experimental error.

By plotting the distance travelled (vertical axis) against the time programmed (horizontal axis) students are able to build up a graph of their data. Students should find that there is a linear (straight line) relationship between the time programmed and the distance travelled. The slope of this line is the velocity of the robot (distance/time).

A random power level between 50% and 100% is assigned to each group, resulting in different results for each group. They cannot copy another group's data as it would be inaccurate for their robot.

This data was taken for the standard DomaBot running at 8.2V battery power. Lower battery levels will change the speed of the robot so ensure that all data is gathered in one session, using the same robot each time.

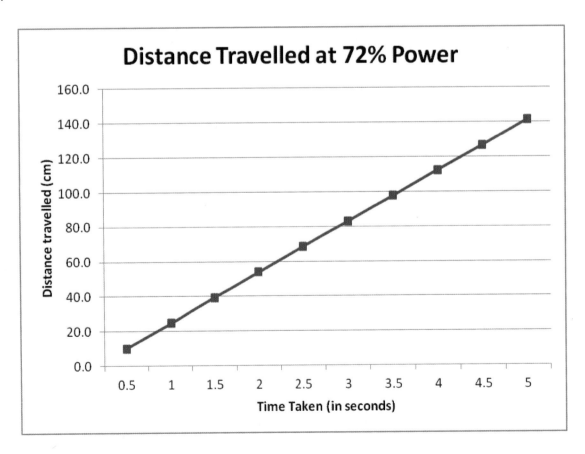

Look out for...

To set up, we will need a starting line and a tape measure. Encourage the students to work out what materials they will need and gently push them in the right direction if they miss out on anything.

If this same experiment is run on carpet, students can expect to see a decrease in the distance of the robot due to the additional friction between the castor wheel and the carpet surface. Encourage this line of thought and get the students to run the same experiment, the same power level on multiple surfaces.

To test that the graph is correct, place an object a random distance away from the starting line. Students will then need to read off their graph through either interpolation (reading within the graph) or extrapolation (reading beyond the graph) to determine the amount of time required to reach the marker. As an added parameter, require the robots to drive up to the marker but not knock it over.

Eg. Place a drink bottle 120cm (47 inches) away. Looking at the graph above, the DomaBot robot would require approximately 4.25 seconds to reach that distance. All groups will have constructed their graphs with different power levels and as such all groups should have a different time requirement.

Example Programs

Make your robot drive forward for 2.5 seconds at 72% power

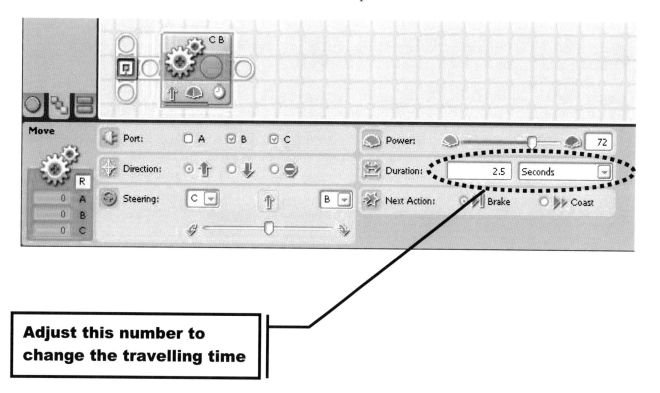

Adjust this number to change the travelling time

Chapter 6:

How fast?

Overview: Test the robot for speed and velocity characteristics

Project: To accurately be able to command the robot, you need to understand how fast it can go and what properties may change its performance. NASA have requested a detailed report, supported by data that you have gathered from your robot.

Equipment required

- 1 NXT robot kit per group
- 1 computer per group
- Masking tape
- Tape measure
- Stopwatch

Teachers Notes

This section does not require any additional software knowledge. All activities can be performed with the use of just the **Move** block. The DomaBot is used to perform data gathering and scientific analysis.

Photocopy and hand out Student Worksheet – How Fast?.

This section will cover the following topics

- Data gathering
- Graphing
- Interpolation / Extrapolation
- Decimal numbers and fractions
- Averaging of data
- Speed and Velocity of a moving body

Theory

Students will need to understand the nature of speed and velocity. The speed of the robot is given as the distance travel within a specified time. This may take on a number of forms such as kilometres per hour, meters per second, feet per second etc.

The speed of the robot will be dependent on the power level as well as the weight of the robot. A heavier robot will take longer to complete the 5 rotations than a lighter robot. If we are using the DomaBot, we should find that a duration of 5 rotations will allow the robot to move a reasonable distance to measure.

Encourage the students to take multiple runs and take the average of all their data to reduce the impact of any experimental error.

When plotting this data, the students will find that there is not a straight line relationship between the power level and the time taken to complete 5 rotation of the wheel. The student will have to sketch out a curve to best fit their data. The more data points we can gather, the more accurate we will be to fit the curve.

This data was taken for the standard DomaBot running at 8.2V battery power. Lower battery levels will change the speed of the robot so ensure that all data is gathered in one session, using the same robot each time.

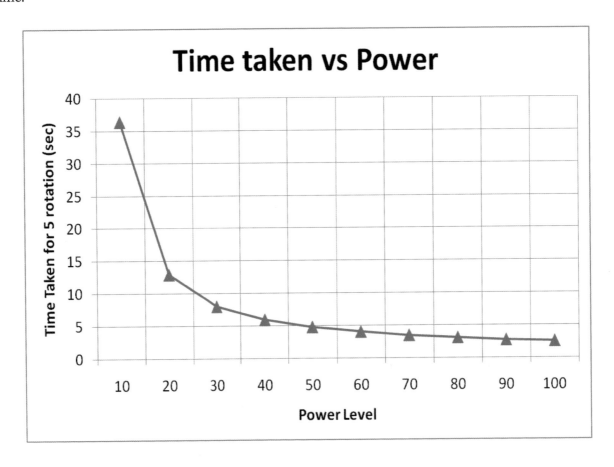

A graph of Speed against Power can be graphed by determining the distance travel over 5 rotations (879mm OR 34.6 inches)

To determine the speed of the robot for each data point, divide the distance travelled over 5 rotations, by the time taken over 5 rotations.

eg.

If our robot takes 8.2 seconds to travel 5 rotations, then the speed can be calculated as follows;

$$\text{speed} = \frac{879 \text{ mm}}{8.2 \text{ seconds}} = \frac{34.6 \text{ inches}}{8.2 \text{ seconds}}$$

$$\text{speed} = 107 \text{ mm/sec} = 4.2 \text{ inches / sec}$$

With this data, students should now find a straight line relationship between speed and power level.

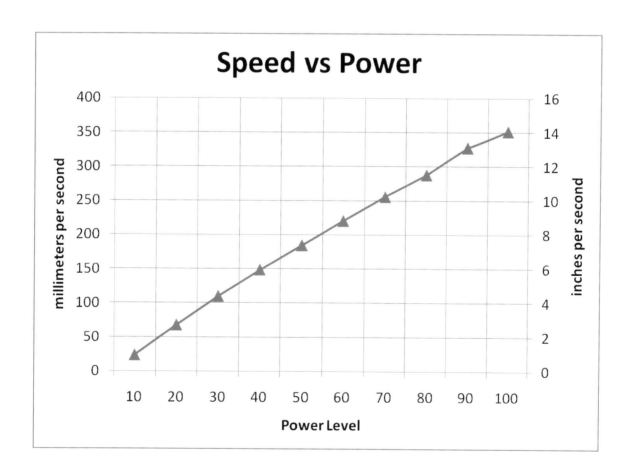

Look out for...

To set up, we will need a starting line a tape measure and a stopwatch. Encourage the students to work out what materials they will need and gently push them in the right direction if they miss out on anything.

When working with a fixed distance as in the case of the first section, we will be able to mark out a finish line as well as a start line. This is useful for students to visually see when the robot reaches 5 rotations rather than stopping the timer when the robot stops.

Smart students will program their robot to drive forward for the 5 rotations, wait a few seconds then reverse back to the start to save the operator from retrieving the robot.

Once they have calculated the speed for their robot, have them run a few tests on an untried power level and check that they do indeed travel at their desired speed. The robot may have a small margin of error

If this same experiment is run on carpet, students can expect to see a decrease in the speed of the robot due to the additional friction between the castor wheel and the carpet surface.

Example Programs

Make your robot drive forward for 5 rotations at 50% power

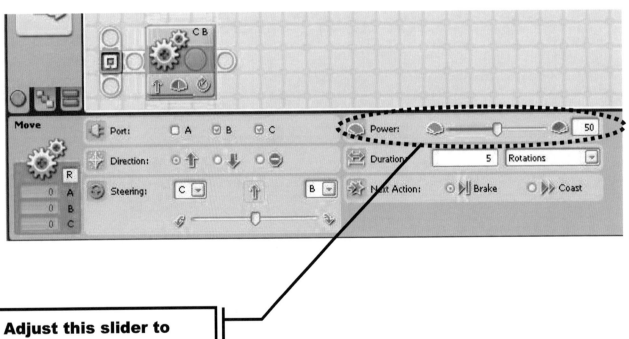

Adjust this slider to change the power level

Extension activity

Build a small platform above the robot that can support the weight of a book. The DomaBot can take up to 2kg in weight if distributed carefully. Students will find that their robot will move considerably slower than before. Run the same set of experiments with this new 'heavier' robot.

Run the same experiments on several different surfaces to investigate the effect of friction on the robot. Good surfaces to test could include:

- Thin carpet
- Thick carpet
- Polished wooded floorboard
- Concrete

Chapter 7:

That bot has personality!

Overview: Use the Sound and Display blocks to give your robot some personality.

Project: NASA are extremely happy with the progress of the project so far, but have asked if it is possible to inject a little personality into your robot. Using the in-built sounds as well as the display screen, it will be possible for the robot to let us know what it is up to!

Equipment Required:

- 1 NXT robot kit per group
- 1 computer per group

Teacher Notes

As well as being a lot of fun, the use of sound and display is an excellent way of 'debugging' programs. By making the robot say a certain phrase at a particular point in the program, students can figure out if it reached that point, just by listening out for it. Eg. Suppose we wanted the robot to perform an elaborate sequence of movements to reach a particular position, we might be looking at 10 or more blocks. A mistake in any of these blocks will follow through to all the other blocks. If we put in a sound effect after the 5th block, students can then use that as a reference point to figure out if they need to make corrections before or after that point.

NXT-G Specific

The LEGO MINDSTORMS system is typically used for robotics and automation applications, but it can also make a great instrument. Built into the main NXT brick is a small speaker capable of playing different notes and sounds

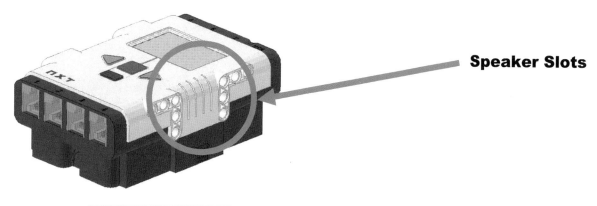

Speaker Slots

You can also change the default sound volume by going through the main menu setting or within the Sound configuration panel itself. A sound level of 4 is the maximum that you can set the NXT.

Setting the default volume

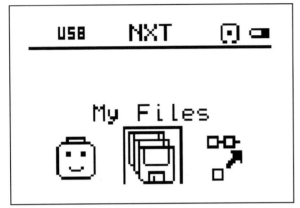

Turn the NXT on

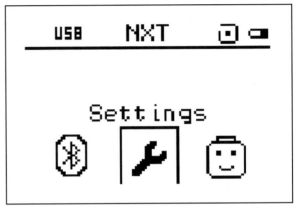

Navigate to the Settings Menu

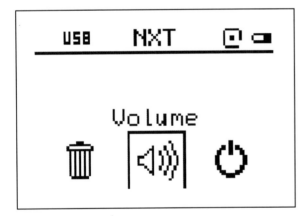

Select the Volume Menu

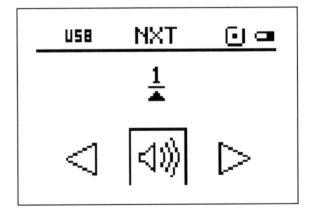

Set the desired Volume

In the Volume Menu, there are 4 different sound levels (1-4). It is also possible to silence the NXT brick by setting a sound level of 0. The MINDSTORMS system is regulated by many standards, one such being the maximum volume permitted for a toy that is used by children. As such, the inbuilt speaker is not extremely loud, but is enough for our purposes.

The Sound Block

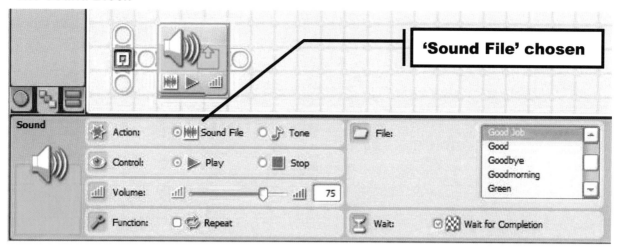

Action: Here we can choose either a pre-loaded sound file or to play an individual tone (note). If we choose the Sound File section, these are the following options available to us.

Control: Just leave this setting on 'Play'.

Volume: Controls the volume.

Function: This asks if we wish to repeat the sound over and over again, in most instances we will leave this unchecked.

File: This is the sound file to use. There are many sound files built into the device already such as 'Good Morning', 'Hooray!' and various buzzes, beeps and clicks.

Wait: If the 'Wait for completion' option is checked, then the program will not move on to the next block until the sound has completely finished.

We also have the ability to play just a specific tone, rather than a pre-recorded sound file. Click on the piano keyboard to select a note and then choose how many seconds you'd like it to play for.

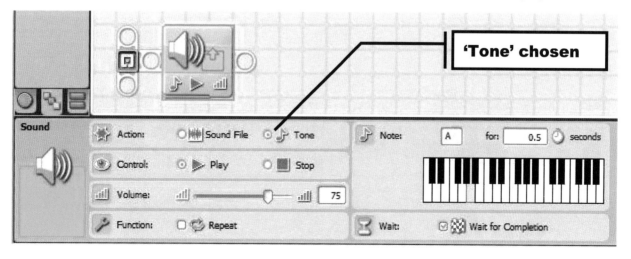

The Display Block

The Display block has two actions that we'll be using the most; Image and Text. The Image action will give you a long file list of pre-drawn images. Get your students to scroll down and find the ones that are most appropriate for their application. The Text option allows us to specify a particular phrase of our own choosing such as 'Take me to your leader!' or "Do you have any bananas?". Use the mouse in the 'Position' option to move the display around.

As with the Sound block, the Display block is an excellent way for students to keep track of where in the program their robot is current at. Eg. Have your robot display on the screen a smiley face when it is driving forward, and a frowning face when it is driving backwards.

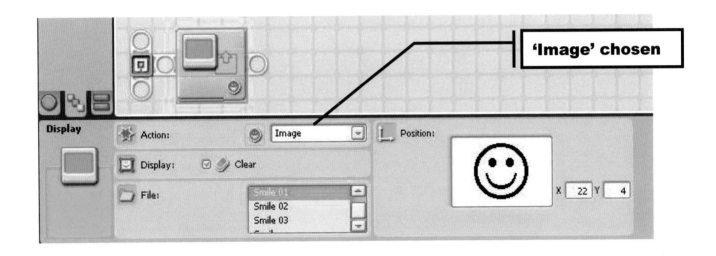

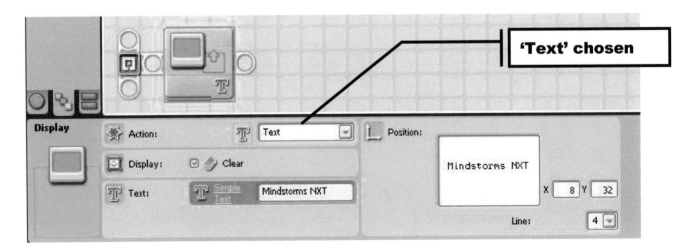

Look out for...

One of the common problems students encounter is when placing a display block right at the very end of a program. As there is no set time for the Display to last, a Display block as the very last instruction will show up for a fraction of a second before the program ends. By adding in a 'Wait for Time' block we can leave that message up for a specific length of time.

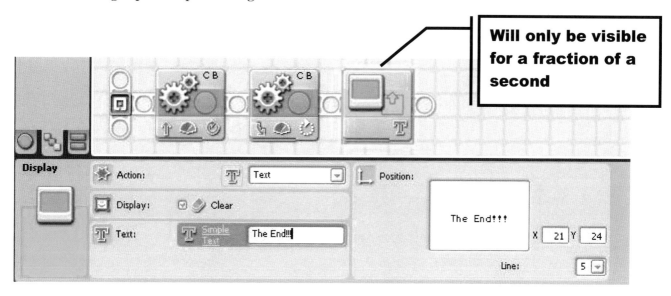

Will only be visible for a fraction of a second

Ensures our 'Display' Block remains visible for a specific time

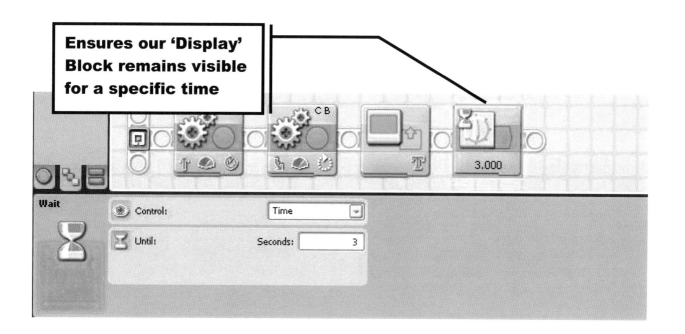

Chapter 8:

How many sides?

Overview: Attach a drawing device to your robot and plot out some geometric shapes.

Project: Once on NXTopia, your robot will be required to identify interesting aspects for later analysis. Your robot will be required to mark off an area such that a passing satellite can easily identify the item in question. Initially you will be required to draw a square, but will then move onto other shapes and designs.

Equipment required:

- 1 NXT robot kit per group
- 1 computer per group
- Large marker
- Large sheet of paper

Teachers Notes

Build the drawing attachment outlined at the end of the book and attach to the front of the robot.

Students will be required to draw a square, but will then move onto other shapes and designs.

This chapter will cover the following topics:

- Basic geometric shapes
- Internal and external angles of a polygon

To draw a square, most students will initially decide to plot out each individual step resulting in 8 blocks (4 sides and 4 corners). But if asked how they would do a hexagon or a triangle, they can be pushed towards understanding the need to repeat sections of code ie." Drive forward and turn, then repeat a certain number of times". This can be achieved with the **Loop** block.

Photocopy and hand out Student Worksheet – How Many Sides?

NXT-G Specific

To make our robot drive in a square, we will need to program it to go forward, turn 90 degrees, go forward, turn 90 degrees, go forward, turn 90 degrees, go forward and do a final 90 degree turn. If we look carefully at the program, we can see that it consists of drive forward, turn 90 degrees and repeated 4 times.

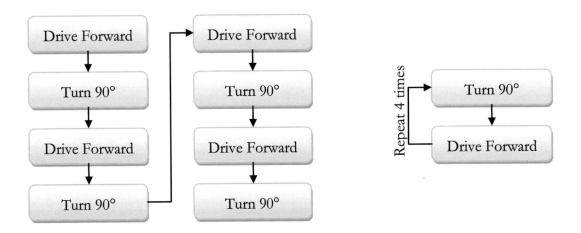

Driving in a square. Which is easier?

We can use the **Loop** block to achieve this simpler form of programming. Everything within the orange border of the **Loop** block will get repeated based on the values in the configuration panel.

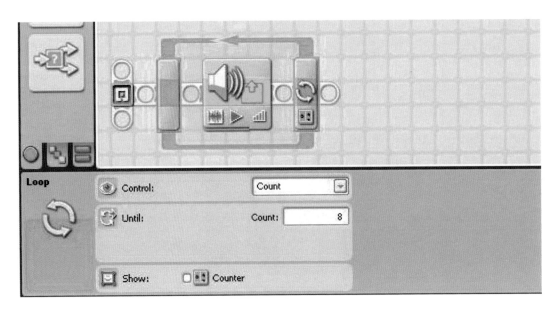

Loop Block: This example program will play a sound file 8 times

Theory

Cumulative error becomes a factor when using the **Loop** block, as errors in the turn angle can build up every time the robot performs the turn. Eg. Let us assume the robot turns 92 degrees instead of 90 degrees. To the human eye, the first turn looks fine, but as the robot progresses around the square, the 2 degree error from each turn is accumulated into an 8 degree error at the end of the square.

When progressing to the octagon, it is important to realise that the angle the robot must turn is the external, or exterior angle of the polygon.

The following equations can be used to calculate the internal and external angles of a polygon.

$$\text{internal angle} = \frac{(\text{number of sides} - 2) \times 180°}{\text{number of sides}}$$

$$\text{external angle} = 180° - \text{internal angle}$$

Shape	Number of sides	Internal angle	External angle	Turn Angle required by the robot*
Octagon	8	135°	45°	135°
Hexagon	6	120°	60°	180°
Triangle	3	60°	120°	360°

*Don't forget that the angle required by the robot, is not the same angle required by the wheel. If the distance between the wheels has changed slightly, then the actual number will be slightly higher or lower than the one indicated in the table.

Refer back to DomaBot Basics to calculate the required durations for the sides of each shape.

Look out for...

The critical component in this challenge is the angle. A robot with the correct turn will arrive exactly back where it started. Mark the starting point with a strip of tape on the floor and measure how close each robot finishes.

With this particular design, the marker is not located at the point from which the centre of the robot will pivot. This will result in the follow shape.

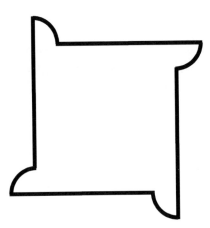

As the marker is located in front of the wheels, the corners will not be perfectly square as indicated in this diagram

Extension Activity

Modifying the mechanical structure of the robot is a good extension activity to run. Have the students change the design of the robot so that it will draw precise corners. This is achieved by locating the marker pen exactly in between the wheels. When the robot turns on the spot, the pen will not travel any distance, and will just rotate over the corner point.

Marker pen needs to be located exactly in between the axis of rotation of the wheels to ensure sharp corners.

Example Program

Make your Robot drive in a square

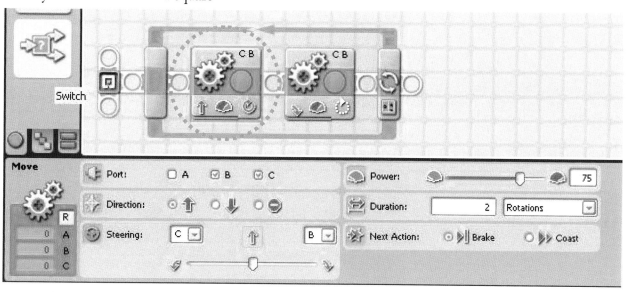

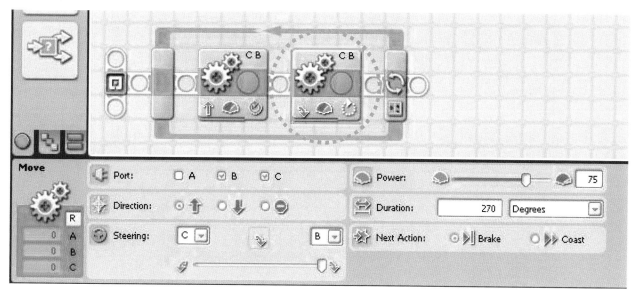

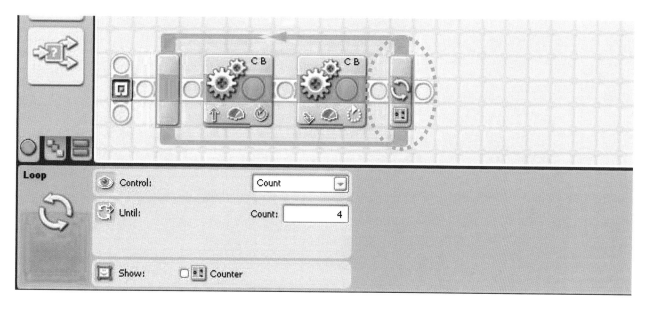

Chapter 9:

Help! I'm Stuck

Overview: Equip your robot with a bump sensor to help it navigate on NXTopia.

Project: Whilst on NXTpoia, your robot will undoubtedly come up against some terrain that is too difficult for the robot to navigate. NASA is worried about a particular chasm near the drop zone where the robot could conceivably get trapped. They have asked that you demonstrate your robots ability to detect such an obstacle and navigate out of the chasm.

Follow the instructions in Building Instructions to construct the touch sensor attachment. Ensure the Touch Sensor cable is connected to Port 1 on the NXT brick.

Equipment required:

- 1 NXT robot kit per group
- 1 computer per group
- Chasm made from books, overturned tables or cardboard boxes

Teachers Notes

Photocopy and hand out Student Worksheet – Help, I'm Stuck. This chapter will introduce students to external sensors on the robot. These sensors can be used to gather information about the environment the robot is in, and with this information the robot can perform informed choices.

Topics covered include

- Complex system
- Sensing and measuring conditions
- Conditional statements

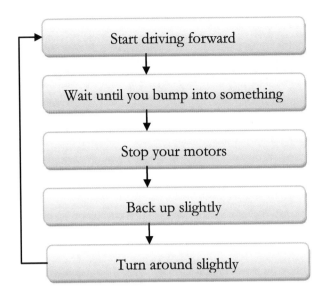

Flowchart outlining possible program flow to solve the Help! I'm stuck challenge

NXT-G Specific

To do this project, we will need to introduce a new set of commands, the **Wait** blocks. These blocks allow us to use the various sensors to control the movement of the motors. The first block we will implement is the **Wait for Touch** block.

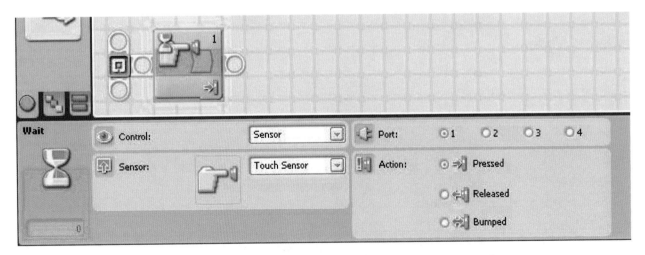

Wait for Touch Block: Wait until the touch sensor has been pressed before moving to the next block

It is best to think of this block as a description. "Wait at this block until the button on Port 1 is pushed. Once the button has been pushed, continue on to the next block."

This activity will also introduce us to another configuration panel parameter within the **Move** block. We do not want our robot to only spin for a set number of revolutions, we want it to spin indefinitely *until* a bump is felt. To make this possible we will use the 'unlimited' option of the duration configuration panel. You will notice a little infinity symbol (∞) appear on the block itself.

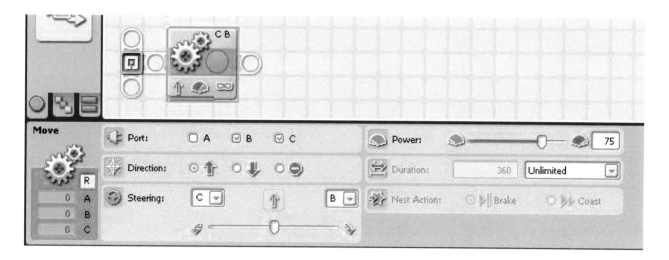

**Turn motors B and C on at a power level of 75 percent,
unlimited duration and move directly to the next block.**

The motor will now continue to spin until it is explicitly turned off by another block.

A good way to think of this is to use the analogy of our lights in our bedroom. If we walk into our room and turn the light switch on, the lights go on. If we now walk out of the room, the lights are still on. If we want the lights to turn off, we must explicitly turn them off. The same is true for motors, if we turn them on with the unlimited option, later on in our program we must use another block to turn them off.

We will be using the unlimited function of the move block for this project. This property allows us to continue driving *until* we are told otherwise. We may have to drive forward half a rotation it may be 10 rotations before we encounter an obstacle. We must wait until the touch sensor has been triggered before we perform any different movements of the robot.

Theory

Senses are what makes a robot a robot, and not a glorified remote control car. With the information gathered by these sensors, the robot can perform an informed decision as to its next movement. Information is recorded from a physical property (ie getting bumped or registering a particular light level) and converted into a stream of data that is meaningful to the brains of the robot.

A conditional statement makes decisions on the flow of the program based on external information. In this challenge, we have asked our robot to drive forward continuously until a particular condition is met. In this case it is when the bump sensor detects a wall. Once this condition is met, the robot can then decide to perform additional actions to deal with the information it has received, namely backing up and turning away.

Look out for...

Students will find that if they just try and turn when they detect a wall, they will get caught up against the wall. A more robust solution will require the robot to back up a small distance before rotating.

The chasm can be as simple as a set of books piled up, or can be built and painted by the students as part of the creative design component of their syllabus.

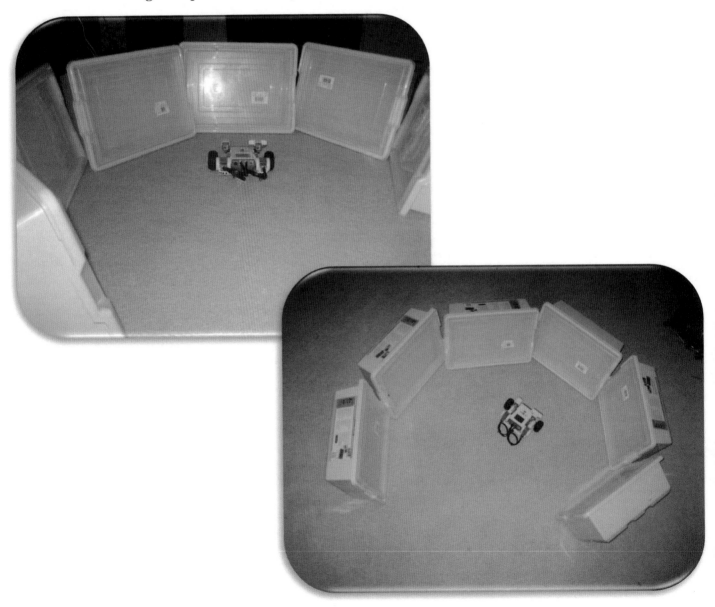

Simple chasm made from NXT storage boxes

Example program

This is a possible solution to the final activity on the worksheet

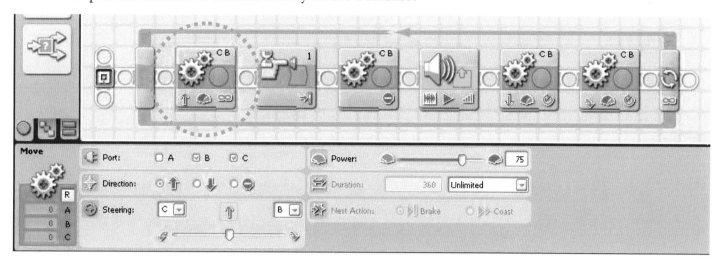

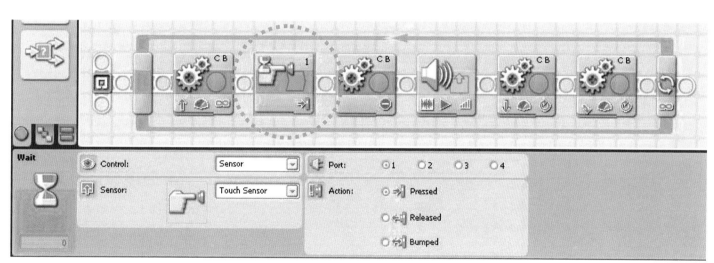

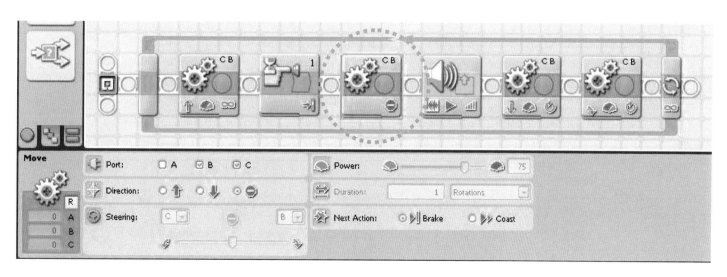

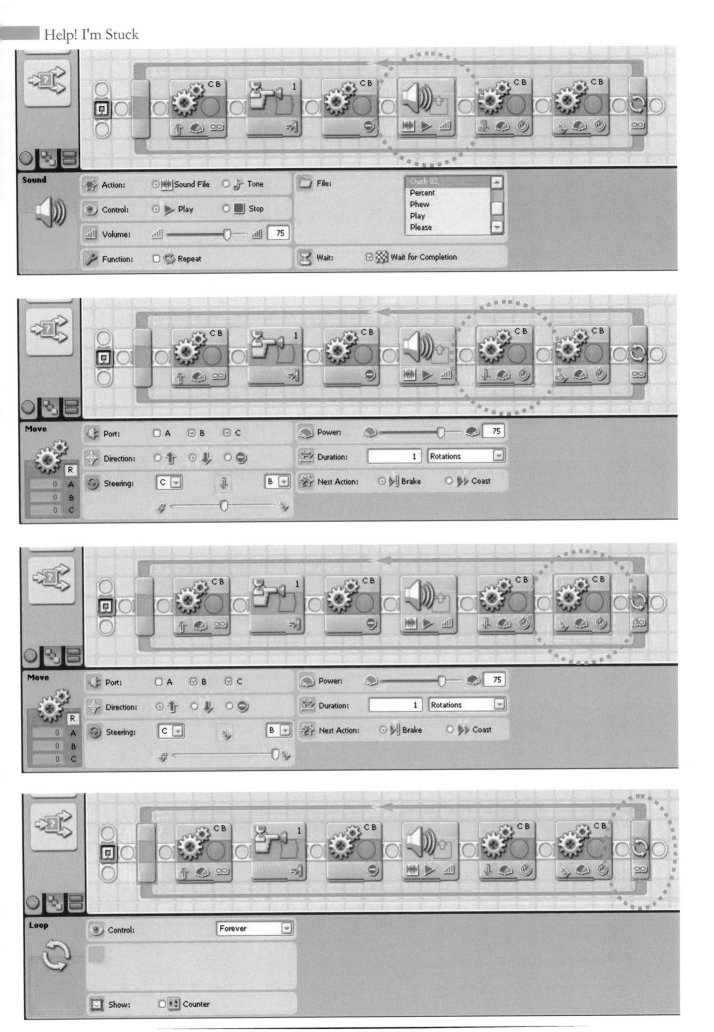

Sound

Action: ⊙ Sound File ○ Tone File: Ouch 02 / Percent / Phew / Play / Please

Control: ⊙ ▷ Play ○ ■ Stop

Volume: 75

Function: ☐ Repeat Wait: ☑ Wait for Completion

Move

Port: ☐ A ☑ B ☑ C Power: 75

Direction: ○ ↑ ⊙ ↓ ○ ⊖ Duration: 1 Rotations

Steering: C ▽ B ▽ Next Action: ⊙ ▷| Brake ○ ▷▷ Coast

R / 0 A / 0 B / 0 C

Move

Port: ☐ A ☑ B ☑ C Power: 75

Direction: ⊙ ↑ ○ ↓ ○ ⊖ Duration: 1 Rotations

Steering: C ▽ B ▽ Next Action: ⊙ ▷| Brake ○ ▷▷ Coast

R / 0 A / 0 B / 0 C

Loop

Control: Forever

Show: ☐ Counter

Chapter 10:

Help! I'm (still) stuck

Project: Swap the bump sensor for the Ultrasonic sensor.

Scenario: NASA are happy with your bumper, but are concerned that the physical impact with the chasm walls will dislodge rocks sitting above. Modify your robot to include the Ultrasonic Sensor and run the same program, but this time recognising the walls before you touch them.

Remove the Touch Sensor attachment and connect a sensor cable from the Ultrasonic Sensor to Port 4 on the NXT brick.

Ensure the Ultrasonic Sensor is connected to Port 4

Teachers Notes

Photocopy and handout Student Worksheet – Help, I'm (still) Stuck.

Students will now need to remove the Touch Sensor attachment from their robot. Make the cables are correctly inserted. As will be explained in the theory below, the values obtained by the Ultrasonic Sensor is highly dependent on the surface of the object that is being detected.

The terminology of Distance and Ultrasonic are often mistakenly interchanged. The correct definition is that the Ultrasonic Sensor is used to measure distance. Within the NXT-G development environment, we will often come across blocks such as **Wait for Distance**, which uses the Ultrasonic sensor to return a distance reading.

This challenge is very similar to the original Help! I'm Stuck challenge and as such requires only a minor modification to the flowchart.

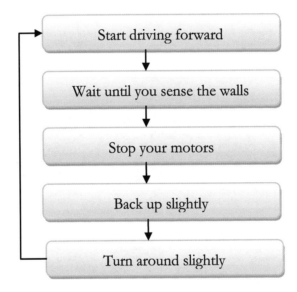

Flowchart outlining possible program flow to solve the Help! I'm (still) stuck challenge

NXT-G Specific

Students will need to swap the **Wait for Touch** block for the **Wait for Distance** block.

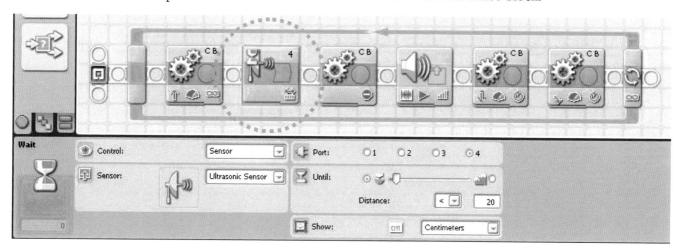

To see what distance values the robot is sensing, we will need to use the view menu on our NXT. The view menu will allow the students to see what values the robot is sensing for each sensor.

Turn the NXT on, you should have the following menu screen. (your robot may not be named 'Damien')

Using the grey left and right arrow button on the NXT, navigate to the 'View' menu item. Press the orange 'select' button to choose the 'View' menu.

Again use the grey left and right arrow buttons to find the 'Ultrasonic cm' or 'Ultrasonic inch' menu. Press the orange button to select this menu.

Choose the correct port that the sensor is plugged into. This will be Port 4 if you have followed the DomaBot building instructions.

The screen will now display a reading for how far away the nearest object is thought to be.

Theory

The Ultrasonic sensor employs the use of ultrasonic range finding to determine to distance to an object. Ultrasonic sensors, or SONAR (SOund Navigation And Ranging) sensors emit a very high frequency soundwave from one of the two openings in the sensor. This soundwave is typically 40KHz, far above what a human ear can detect. This soundwave travels through the air, and bounces off an object with the echo returning to the other opening on the sensor. By measuring how long it has taken for the sound to travel out to the object and return again, the sensor can determine how far away the object is.

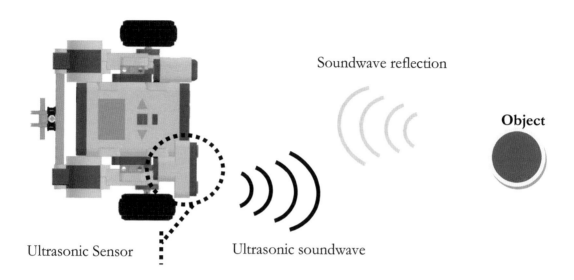

Soundwave reflection

Object

Ultrasonic Sensor

Ultrasonic soundwave

The robot is able to determine the distance to the object by timing how long it takes a reflected soundwave to return to the sensor.

The reading that the Ultrasonic sensor will display is dependent on the surface off which the ultrasonic waveform is reflected. Smooth, perpendicular surfaces give accurate readings, whereas irregular surfaces, (such as hands, other robots, angled walls etc) may give different results. The key here is to do plenty of testing.

Look out for...

Students must also remember that the distance measure of the sensor if taken from the front of the sensor, which may not be the front of the robot. Make sure they take into account any attachment sitting in front of the robot.

Students will find that the readings they get from their sensor do not match what they are able to measure with a ruler. This is a result of the ultrasonic waveform bouncing off the intended object at unusual angles.

If the cable has not been correctly connected on the robot, or it has been connected to the wrong port, you will see the following screen when trying to view the Ultrasonic sensor readings.

**Cable not correctly plugged in, cable plugged into the wrong sensor port
or nearest object is too far away to be seen.**

Example Program

See the example programs for Help! I'm Stuck, and substitute in the **Wait for Distance** block in place of
the **Wait for Touch** block.

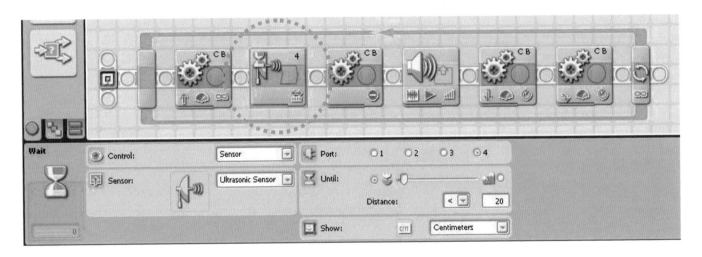

Wait for Distance Block: Wait at this block until the distance measured by the Ultrasonic sensor in Port 4
gives a reading of less than 20 cm. Once this condition has been met, proceed directly to the next block.

Chapter 11:

Stay Away from the Edge

Overview: Use the light sensor to remain on the table.

Project: Another challenge the robot might face is safe navigation along a ridge line. Get too close and over you go. NASA has asked that you prove your robot is capable of staying away from the edge of a cliff.

Equipment required:

- 1 NXT robot kit per group
- 1 computer per group
- Table top

Teachers Notes

Follow the instructions in Building Instructions, to attach the light sensor attachment to the robot.

The algorithm for this particular challenge is very similar to the previous challenge, but using the light sensor in place of either the touch or Ultrasonic sensor. The light sensor is arrange such that it is looking straight down at the table. This will return a high reading whilst on the table, and will transition to a significantly lower reading once the light sensor has gone over the edge of the table. Once this change in light reading has been observed, the robot can then stop the motors, preventing it from going over the edge of the table.

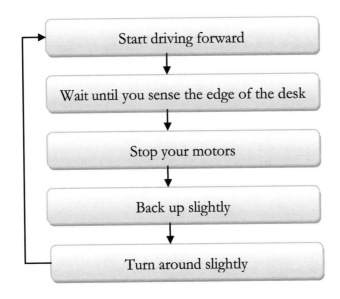

**Flowchart outlining possible program flow to solve the
Stay Away from the Edge challenge**

NXT-G Specific

This challenge requires the use of the Light Sensor block.

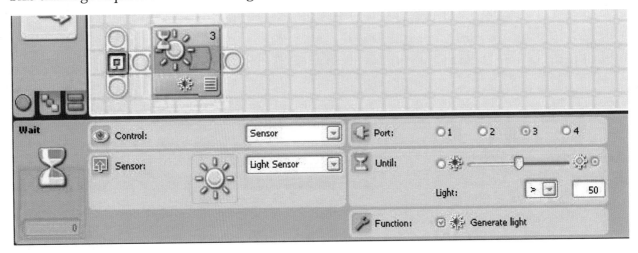

The **Wait for Light** block operates in the same fashion as the **Wait for Touch** and **Wait for Distance** blocks. The block can be configured to wait for either the situation where the light levels are increasing or when the light levels are decreasing.

Theory

The *threshold* is a term that is used to differentiate between two different states. All the information that the NXT receives is converted into numbers so it is understandable by the robot. By selecting a *threshold*, it is possible for the robot to decide if it is either 'above' or 'below' this threshold.

Take for example the robot driving on a white piece of paper towards a black line. As the sensor passes over the black line, the light sensor readings will not just change from a high number to a low number, instead it will side down the readings until it reaches the value for solid black. These 'in between' numbers are still valid readings and the robot must decide if they are either 'white' or 'black'; it has no sense of 'grey'.

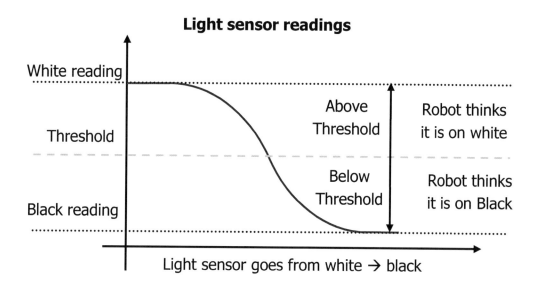

Let us assume that when on the white paper, the robot's light sensor gives us a reading of 50. When on the black, it gives a reading of 30. What we need to decide is, at what number (our threshold) does our robot go from seeing white to seeing black? The safest number to choose is halfway in between, 40. If our sensor reads above 40, it is a very good chance that we are on white. If we are below 40, then chances are we are on black. This number can be push a little higher or lower and this will cause the robot to react a little faster or a little slower to the black line.

Look out for...

Choosing a threshold value works best when there is considerable contrast between the table and the floor.

Good: White shiny table with a dark carpet. This setup will give high readings for the table and low readings for when the sensor is over the edge of the desk.

Not so Good: White table over polished wood with lots of sunlight in the room. The sunlight will bounce off the shiny floor and straight into the sensor. It is possible in some circumstances to have the edge of the desk brighter than the desk itself. If necessary, place a white sheet over the table for added contrast.

The major problems the students will encounter are as follows

Problem: Robot does not react to the edge of the table.

- Possible Solution: Threshold value is not a number in between the light and dark readings. Take some new readings and calculate a new threshold number
- Possible Solution: If the students hold their hands too close to the robot in anticipation of catching, the robot will believe the hands are an extension of the desk and will continue to drive.

Problem: Robot only drives forward a small amount before stopping, although the program still appears to be running.

- Possible Solution: The first move block has not be set to unlimited. What has most likely occurred is that the robot has driven forward 1 rotation as directed and is now sitting still waiting for the light sensor value to go low.
- Check to ensure the **Wait for Light** is configured for 'less than'. If it is configured for 'greater than', the robot takes a reading of the table, realises it is already greater than the threshold and stops immediately.

Problem: Robot recognises the edge but falls off as it turns.

- Possible Solution: Back the robot up further before attempting to turn around.

Example Program

This program is the same as 'Help, I'm stuck', but uses the **Wait for Light** block instead of the other **Wait** blocks.

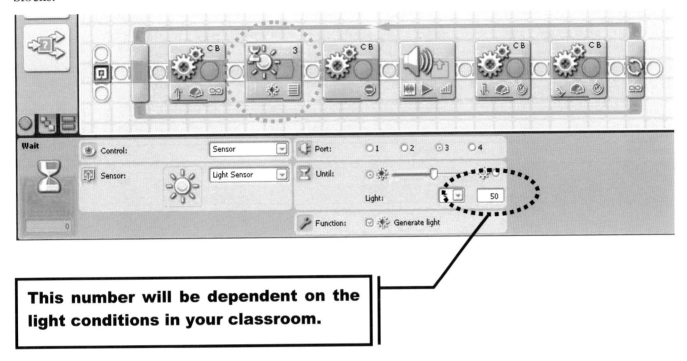

This number will be dependent on the light conditions in your classroom.

Extension Activities

This particular challenge can be used anywhere there are two contrasting colours present. These activities are all appropriate.

- White masking tape 'prison' on a dark carpet
- Black electrical tape 'maze' on white tiles

Chapter 12:

Did you hear that?

Overview: Use the Sound sensor to react to noise.

Project: The possibility of alien life forms present on NXTopia is quite high. NASA are concerned that they might be hiding and that the robot will not see them unless it can hear them approaching. Build a robot that can react to loud sounds.

Remove the Light Sensor attachment from the previous challenge. Connect the Sound Sensor to Port 2 on the NXT brick.

Ensure the Sound Sensor is connected to Port 2

Equipment required:

- 1 NXT robot kit per group
- 1 computer per group

Teachers Notes

Students will have to use the 'view' menu item to take different readings of loud and quiet sounds. A short sharp clap, close to the microphone will likely take the sensor to its upper threshold of 100. When choosing a threshold, keep it quite high (over 85) so that the robot will only respond to a noise that is generated close to the robots sensor. When you have a class of many robots, it can get quite noisy!

Theory

It is important to realise that sound is quite a slow phenomenon when compared to light or touch. The sound of a clap of the hands can last quite a long time.

The following graph shows the sensor readings for a clap.

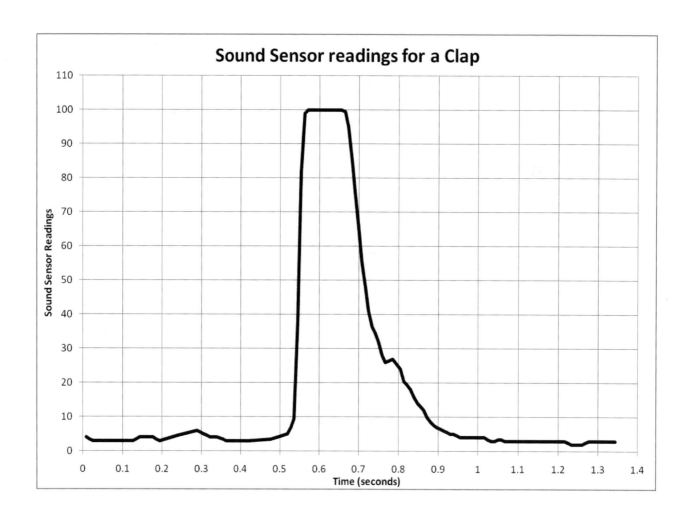

There is very little reading to start with, and then the sensor rapidly climbs just after 0.5 second. The sensor maxes out at a reading of 100 for approximately 0.1 of a second before it falls again.

This can become problematic when using the sound sensor to differentiate between different claps.

Take the following program, where we want the robot to start moving with a clap, and stop moving with a clap.

Clap to start moving, clap to stop moving. Will not work!

This particular implementation will not work, as the first clap will trigger the first **Wait for Sound** block, at which point the robot will turn the motors on with an unlimited duration. It will then start listening for the second clap, which in fact is still the first clap as it has not had enough time to die away. Thus this one clap will trigger both **Wait for Sound** blocks.

There are two possible solutions to get around this issue;

Wait for 0.2 seconds after each clap to give the clap time to fade away.

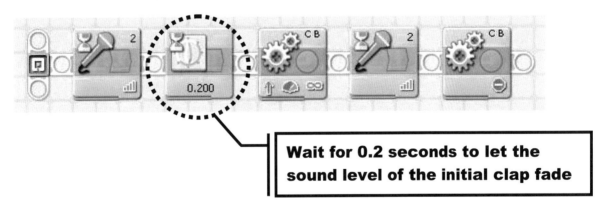

Wait for 0.2 seconds to let the sound level of the initial clap fade

Wait for the measured volume to get loud, and then wait for it to get soft before turning on any motors.

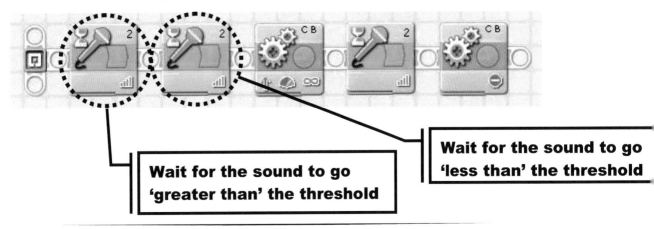

Wait for the sound to go 'greater than' the threshold

Wait for the sound to go 'less than' the threshold

Look out for....

In a large group with many students, you will find that it is easy for other groups to accidentally trigger another group's robot. Wooden floors tend to transmit sound waves very efficiently, with a heavy footstep at one end of the classroom being recognised by a robot at the other end of the room.

Be aware that the motors also make noise, and while it is not loud enough to be a concern for this particular challenge, if the students wish to trigger on quieter sounds, they must take into account this extra noise.

Example programs

Drive forward until you hear a sound and then stop for 2 seconds and slowly turn around for 360 degrees of the robot.

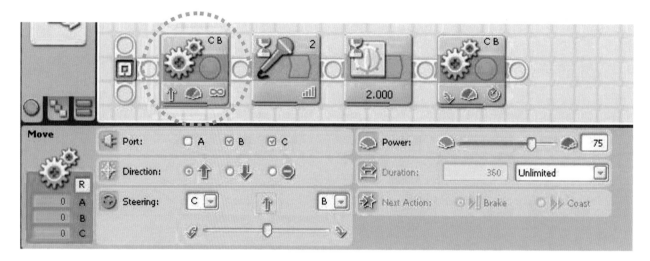

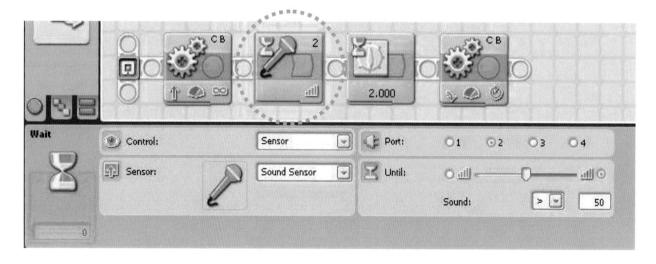

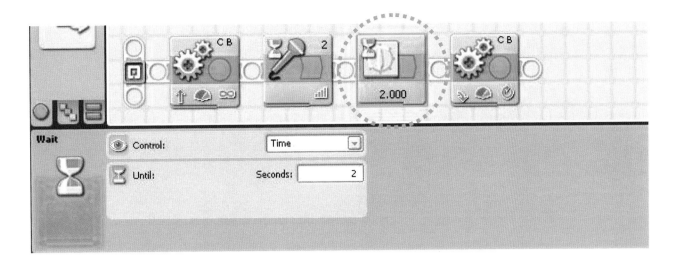

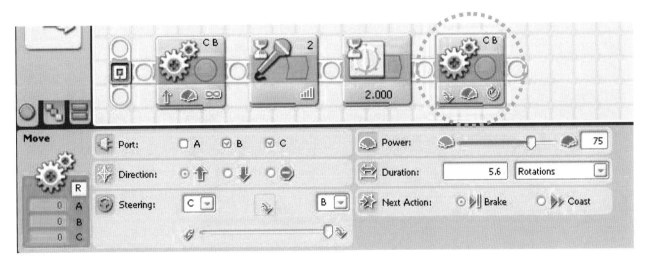

Chapter 13:

Mini-Golf

Overview: Build and program a robot to play a round of mini-golf.

Project: Students use the skills they have learnt from previous weeks to build a robot that can play a game of mini golf.

Equipment required:

- 1 NXT robot kit per group
- 1 computer per group
- Red and Blue NXT ball
- Putting green (see below)

Set up:

A putting green is required with a set cup location. This could be constructed with a sheet of MDF or plywood. Use a hole saw to cut a 50mm / 2 inch hole in the board to act as the golf cup. Sand down any rough edges.

Print out or paint a bullseye pattern using the following dimensions as a guideline.

- Centre hole: 5cm / 2 inch
- 1st ring: 10cm / 4 inch
- 2nd ring: 20cm / 6 inch
- 3rd ring: 30cm / 10 inch

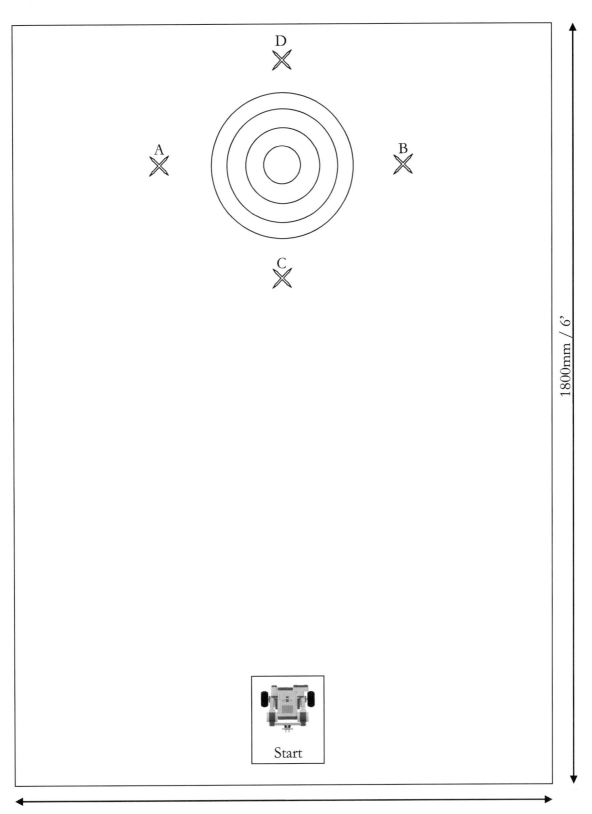

1800mm / 6'

1200mm / 4'

Game Play:

Robot is placed in the starting box.

A standard golf ball is placed in either position A, B, C or D.

Competitor presses the run button and allows the robot to head off.

There are 5 rounds, with the golf ball placed is a different location for each round.

Robots have 1 minutes in which to strike the ball. They may restart as many times as they wish within this time until the ball is struck. Once struck, the final resting position of the ball determines the points scored for the round.

The ball should be struck, not pushed, towards the cup.

Scoring

- 50 points for getting it in the hole
- 30 points for closest ring
- 20 points for the next ring
- 10 points for the outer ring
- 5 points for making contact with the ball

Teachers Notes

The students will need to discover that they need some sort of 'bumper' on the front to ensure accurate and repeatable test runs. Something resembling a slight 'v' shape will probably work best as it will funnel the ball towards the centre of the robot.

Rounds 1 and 2 allow them to get points on the board. Hitting the ball as hard as possible should be naturally discouraged as if they miss the cup, they do not want it rolling completely off the bullseye.

Rounds 3,4 and 5 should promote planning. Ideally they should draw on a piece of paper what path their robot will take, and what movements they need to accomplish it.

Extension Activities

Is it possible to knock in all 4 golf ball locations from a single program? ie. No taking the robot back to the starting position to reset.

Research other mini-golf layouts and replicate some of the interactive elements (windmills, moving characters etc)

Chapter 14:

Dancing Robots

Overview: Program your robot to perform their own dance routine

Project: Students will synchronise multiple robot to dance and move in time with the music. The focus for this challenge is the integration and coordination of multiple robots.

Equipment required:

- 1 NXT robot kit per group
- 1 computer per group
- Music player
- Decorations (straws / pipe cleaners etc)

Teachers Notes

Students can team up with other groups to create dancing partners or they can perform a solo dance.

Choose a piece of music approximately 60 seconds in length

With either a stopwatch or software program, have the students map out the time it takes for significant sections of the music. Once they have the length of times required, they can start programming their robots to fill each time bracket. Test often with the music to ensure the robots movements synchronise with the timing of the music.

When they are happy with their performance, have the student dress up their robots with decorations such as:

- Pipe cleaners
- Coloured paper
- Bobbly eyes
- Sequins
- Feathers

Look out for...

Here are a few tips to make the students robot presentation more visually appealing. The key concept is timing with the music. An entertaining robot dance to watch has the robots changing their movements in time with the music.

Alternate the robots movements between fast and slow motions. The more variety and contrast there is in the performance, the better it is to watch. Do some research into the RoboCup Junior Competition. There is a division devoted to dancing robots with many excellent examples available. Look at the 'Resources' section of the Domabotics website for videos of dancing robots.

The following table is very useful in planning out robots dance sequences.

Song Name:	**'Robots Rock'**	**Artist:**	**The Amazing Androids**
Section	*Time*	*Description*	*Intended robot movement*
Intro	0 sec – 8 sec	Slow and steady. Just drums and bass guitar	Slow rocking from side to side in time with drums
1st Verse	8 sec – 15 sec	Guitars come in and speed gets faster	Looped forward and backwards movements, slightly faster than intro
Chorus	15 sec – 23 sec	Steady rhythm, quite fast	Robots even faster now, doing full turns on the sopt
2nd verse	...	...	...
Chorus			

If you are finding resistance from the students to the concept of 'dancing' robots, the same activity can be performed but with a different theme

- Robotic Marching Band
- Aerial stunt pilots (eg. The Flying Roulettes)
- Synchronised swimming

Keep the movements relatively short. A robot that drives forward for 1 second is actually quite a long time. Keep dance movements short and repeat often. Encourage the students to use up time with the loop command. ie.

[(FORWARD 0.2 seconds, BACKWARD 0.5 seconds, turn clockwise 0.3 second) repeat 5 times]

This particular sequence would take up 5 seconds with only 4 blocks used.

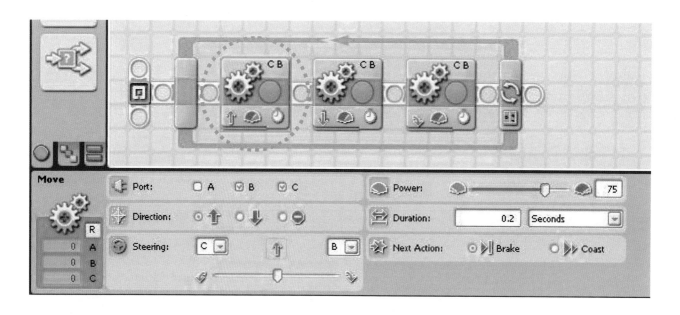

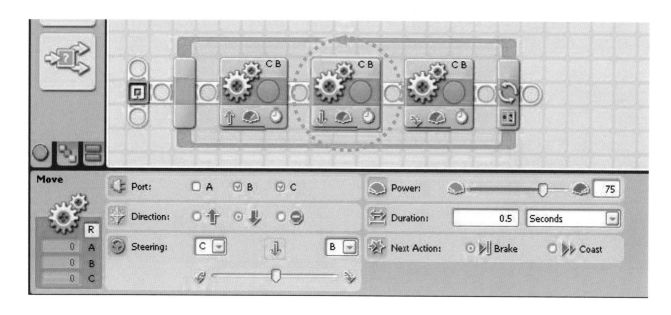

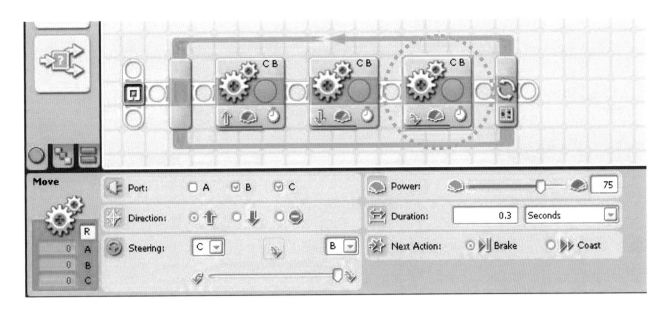

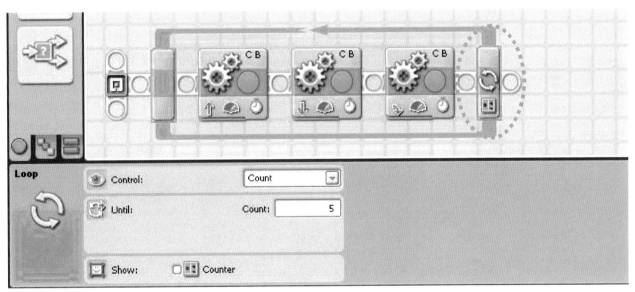

Extension Activity

Create a music video of your robot in action. Take multiple videos of the robots in action. Using movie editing software, cut the different segments together. Add some special effect and the backing music and show it to the class.

Chapter 15:

Robot Wave

Overview: Create your own robotic supporters for the local sporting match

Project: Students will synchronise multiple robot to perform a Robot wave.

Equipment required:

- 1 NXT robot kit per group
- 1 computer per group

Teachers Notes

Students will line their robots up, and on starting, each of the robots will move forward and then move backwards. Individually this program is quite unexciting, but when teamed up with multiple robots, the effect can be very appealing.

The emphasis for this challenge is the coordination of several robots. The program required to do the basic motion is quite straight forward, but the success of the robots is dependent on all robots running at the correct time.

A Robot wave is created in a sporting stadium when a group of people stand up and sit down again. The people immediately to their side do the same and the 'wave' progresses around the stadium.

The basic program to implement a Robot wave is as follows.

- Wait for a set period of time
- Drive forward, 75% power for 1 second
- Drive backward, 75% power for 1 second

The key component is how long each robot is required to wait before heading off. The first implementation should have Robot 1 wait for 0.5 seconds, before driving forward. Robot 2 will wait for 1 second, Robot 3 will wait for 1.5 seconds and so on down the line.

All Robots lined up

First Robot heads off

Second Robot heads off

Third Robot heads off

etc...

When using a 0.5 second delay between each robot, the required 'wait' time is half the group number. eg. Group 5 will need to wait for 2.5 seconds.

Once the initial wave has been mastered, it is possible to extend the range of motions that each robot performs. Rather than the basic 'Drive forward, Drive backward', try these different combinations. Leave it to the group to devise their own choreography.

- Forward 1 second fast, Backward 1 second slow
- Forward 1 second, Backward 2 second, Forward 1 second
- Forward 1 second, Backward 2 second, Forward 1 second, Loop the whole procedure 4 times
- Arrange the robots in a circle rather than a straight line

Example Program

This program describes the basic Robot wave program

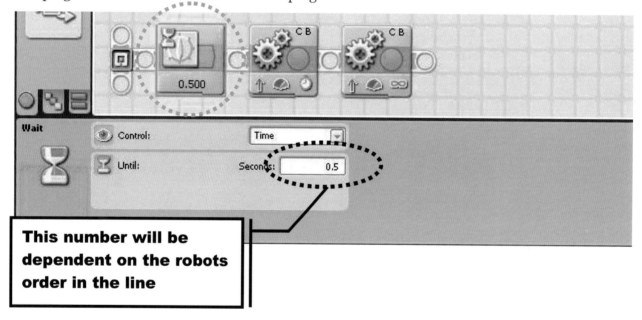

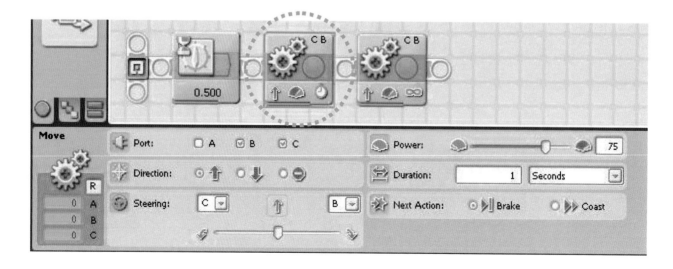

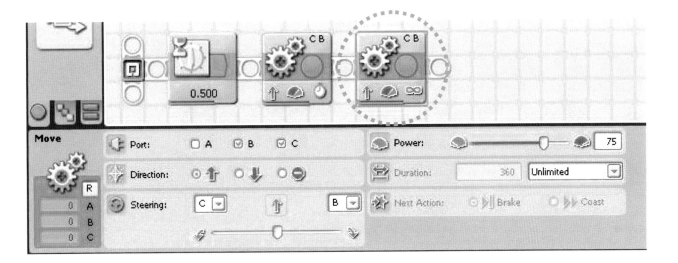

Extension Activities

Can you hear me?

The trickiest part of the Robot Wave challenge is coordinating multiple robot to all run at the same time. This can be bypassed by using the Sound sensor to trigger the robots.

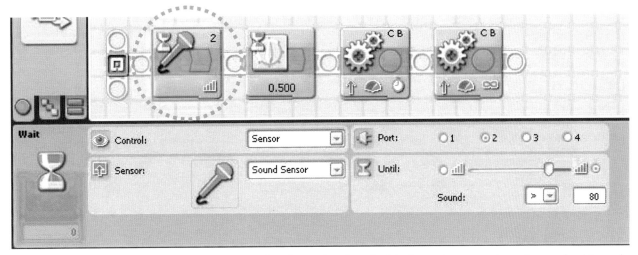

By entering in a relatively high (80+) number into the threshold, the robots can be triggered with a clap or a stamp of the feet. The **Wait for Time** block will need to be retained, otherwise all the robots will move forward in a line once the sound level has been exceeded.

Up and Back

Have the wave progress up the line, and then come back down the line to the starting robot. This will require some careful planning to ensure each robot knows how long to wait before performing their 2nd wave.

Cheerleaders

Add the 3rd motor to the robot to create some arms with pom-poms. Run the Robot wave using these pom-poms as well.

Chapter 16:

Robot Butler

Overview: Build a robot that can assist the elderly and disabled

Project: Robots in the household are quickly becoming commonplace, with personal assistance robots widely regarded to become the most prevalent in the near future. Build a robot that can retrieve a drink for someone who is confined to bed.

Teachers Notes

This challenge can be as open ended as required. There is no extra content that is required to be taught, rather the challenge is in integrating the various systems and programming knowledge that has already been learnt.

A typical scenario is as follows.

> *Your great Aunt Winnifred is confined to her bed due to her bad ankle. You are required to build a robot that can fetch a glass of water from the kitchen and return it to her bedside.*
>
> *It must navigate from the bedroom, out the door and down the hallway to the kitchen on the left hand side. Once the robot is in the kitchen, it must drive up to within 5cm / 2" of the shelf. A drink is placed on the top of the robot and it must return to the bedroom.*

For this challenge student will be required to accurately plan a path out of the bedroom and down to the kitchen using the **Move** block. Once there, they then use the Ultrasonic sensor to approach the shelf. Students will need to build a platform on which to hold the cup of water (empty of course). This platform could use the touch sensor to tell when a weight has been placed on the robot. Once the cup is on the robot, it must turn around and return to the bedroom.

This can be as open ended as desired and the scenario can be tailored to suit any ability or theme within the classroom.

Variations

Race Car

The robot must navigate a race car track, but also stop at the pit stop for fuel and wait until other cars to leave the pit stop before exiting.

Traffic Lights

Robot must traverse down a suburban street and stop for traffic lights and pedestrians.

Rubbish Disposal

Robots drive around a table top and when they find a piece of trash, they take it to the edge of the table and dispose of it over the side.

Chapter 17:

As seen on TV!

Overview: Create a multimedia presentation to market and sell your robot.

Project: NASA have decided on using your design to fly to NXTopia. As a result of the associated publicity, many other people want to buy their own version of the robot. Come up with a marketing promotion to sell your robot.

Equipment required:

- 1 NXT robot kit per group
- 1 computer per group

Teachers Notes

Students should think of their group as a 'company' that must pitch a 'product' (in this case their robot) to the general public. It is left up to the teacher to decide the final format, but any of the following media types would be appropriate.

- School Newspaper article
- Video commercial
- PowerPoint Presentation
- Poster presentation
- Website
- Oral Presentation

Students can have considerable leeway with the creative claims of their product as long as they are feasible.

Good – Our robot can be charge by solar panels

Bad – Our robot can fly just by driving very fast!

Issue that will need to be addressed include:

- Form – What does it look like?
- Function – What can it do?
- How does it move?
- How does it sense its environment?
- How much will it cost?
- Are there any special features?

Chapter 18:

Meet your adoring public!

Overview: After your glorious mission, your robot will want to meet with its fans and supporters

Project: Program your robot to respond in a positive way when somebody gets close. Use the **Move**, **Sound** and **Display** blocks to convey a feeling of happiness.

Equipment required:

- 1 NXT robot kit per group
- 1 computer per group

Teacher Notes

This project can be built up in stages. Initially just have the student's robot respond when somebody walks up to it. This is similar to the "Help! I'm (still) stuck" activity in the use of the Ultrasonic Sensor. But in this case, rather than waiting for the robot to drive up to an object, it will wait for an object to approach itself. Once the robot can accurately identify an object, students can then let their creative energies flow to have their robot respond with a feeling of happiness. 'Happiness' is a very subjective measure and it is always interesting to see what interpretation the students come up with.

Example Program

This program waits until somebody approaches within 30 cm (12 inches), says 'Good morning!" and then does a little wiggle. The whole time it has a smiley face on the display.

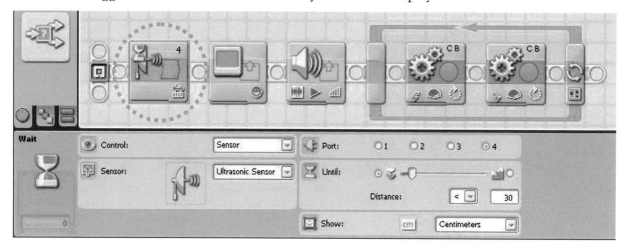

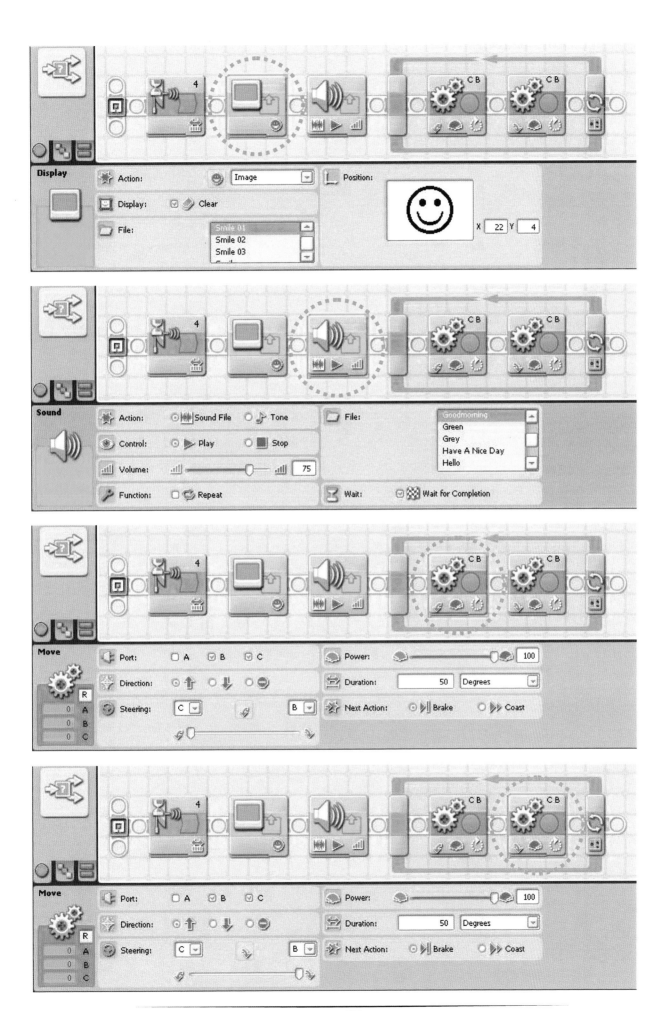

Display

Action: Image

Display: ☑ Clear

File:
Smile 01
Smile 02
Smile 03

Position:
X 22 Y 4

Sound

Action: ◉ Sound File ○ Tone

Control: ◉ ▶ Play ○ ■ Stop

Volume: 75

Function: ☐ Repeat

File:
Goodmorning
Green
Grey
Have A Nice Day
Hello

Wait: ☑ Wait for Completion

Move

Port: ☐ A ☑ B ☑ C

Direction: ◉ ↑ ○ ↓ ○ ⊝

Steering: C B

Power: 100

Duration: 50 Degrees

Next Action: ◉ ▶‖ Brake ○ ▶▶ Coast

R
0 A
0 B
0 C

Move

Port: ☐ A ☑ B ☑ C

Direction: ◉ ↑ ○ ↓ ○ ⊝

Steering: C B

Power: 100

Duration: 50 Degrees

Next Action: ◉ ▶‖ Brake ○ ▶▶ Coast

R
0 A
0 B
0 C

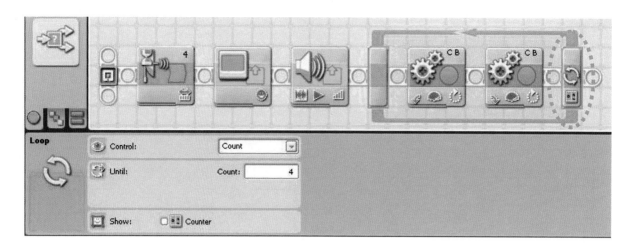

Extension Activity

The natural extension to this project is to now have the robot act 'sad' when the person walks away. To implement this, you will again need a 'Wait for Distance' block, but this time the robot is waiting for a **Greater Than** condition to occur as the person walks away. It is advisable that you increase the threshold distance as your robot may have moved from its initial starting position when it does its 'happy' movements. Sad actions generally include sad faces, low notes and slow movements.

Add a third motor to the 'A' port and connect a flag for a true parade loving robot!

Chapter 19:

Student Worksheets

In this section you will find all the student worksheets referred to in the preceding chapters. The owner of this book has photocopy permission to reproduce as many copies of these worksheets as is required by their class.

Student Worksheet – What is a Robot?

When you hear the word 'robot' some famous movie robots spring to mind. Robots in real life however are not yet up to the standard of their movie counterparts.

Robots are becoming more prevalent in today's society. There are used in high level applications such as space exploration right through to commercial vacuuming robots found in everyday households. You are required to do a research assignment on robotics in general and to focus on one robot in particular.

Robots come in many different shapes and sizes and are often tailored to meet a particular need or action.

Assessment

Create a report on robotics. Your teacher will tell you the format of the report. The following questions will need to be addressed in your work.

- What is a robot?
- Why do we have robots?
- Name some different types of robots?
- What are the main components of a robot?
- Where did the term 'Robot' come from?

Pick one robot and elaborate on it. You must have your robot choice approved by your teacher before you start your research. You will need to include the following information in your report:

Sensors - What information does it take in? (e.g. Sound, distance etc)

Software - What does it do? (e.g. Vacuum floors, explore space)

Mechanical - What materials is it made out of? How does it move? (e.g. motors, arms and metal frames)

Robot Chosen _____   Due Date_____

Presentation Type_____   Page / Slide limit_____

Student Worksheet - Flowcharting

All robots need to have programs to make them run. The easiest way to start a program is to firstly have a plan. This plan consists of a flowchart of small steps that make up the entire program. Each step is simple enough that the robot can perform it without too much effort.

Task: Using the blank flowchart below, plan out your daily morning routine, from when you wake up until you get to school.

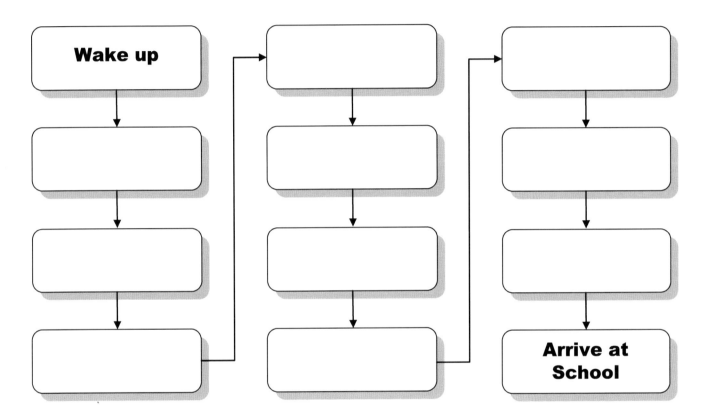

Student Worksheet – DomaBot Basics

Group Name_____   Group Members_____

Overview: NASA is in the market for a new planetary rover to explore the recently discover planet NXTopia.   You are required to design and construct a robot that is capable of following a set of commands to explore the planet's surface.   Before the robot is deployed, it must be extensively tested to ensure it will perform as expected.   You can't fly a technician to NXTopia to reboot the robot!

Before we send our robot into space, we must first test it thoroughly here on earth.   Run the following experiments and observe how your robot behaves.   Do not move to the next experiment until your teacher has seen your current experiment.

Drive Forward for 90° of the wheels
How far did your robot travel?   _____

Drive Forward for 0.25 rotations of the wheels
How far did your robot travel?   _____

What is the circumference of the robots wheel?
          (hint: you will need to measure the diameter of the wheel)   _____

How far will the robot drive if the wheels turn 3 rotations?   _____

Program your robot to move 3 rotations and measure how far it goes.
Does it go as far as you expected?

Drive Forward 540° slow, then 540° back as fast as possible

Turn the robot around 180°
What happened? How far did your robot turn if you type in 180°?   _____

How much Duration does the wheel need for the robot to turn 180°?
          (hint: keep experimenting until it is perfect!)   _____

Drive forward for 500mm (OR 20 inches), turn around 180° and drive back to where you started

How much duration do you need to go forward 500mm (20 inches)?

> (hint: Have a look at the circumference of your wheel,
> this will tell you how far your robot goes in 1 rotation)   _____

Make your robot drive in a 'figure of 8'

(hint: draw a diagram first in the space below before you start programming. Don't forget to mark your starting point!)

Student Worksheet – How far?

Group Name_____   Group Members_____

Overview: In the initial construction of the robot the travelling characteristics are required.   After characterising the properties, NASA have asked that you use your data to make predictions about the distance your robot will travel given specific time constraints.

Your group will be assigned a random power level to be assessed.   Power Level Assigned _____

For this experiment you will need to measure how far the robot travels for different time values (eg. 1 second, 2 seconds, 3.5 seconds etc).   The more data you gather, the more accurate your graph will be.

Plot the results either on the graph below or in a graphing software package.

(Hint: you will need to know the smallest and largest times you tested for, as well as the smallest and largest distances so that you can determine the horizontal and vertical axis scales)

Once you have plotted your data, can you see a relationship between the time taken and the distance travelled?

By looking at the graph, can you determine how many seconds
your robot would need to travel exactly 30com (12 inches)?   _____ seconds

How about 1.5m (59 inches)?   _____ seconds

Your teacher will assign you a test distance. How long does your robot need to travel this particular distance?

Test Distance = _____   Time required = _____ seconds

Distance Travelled vs Time Taken

Distance Travelled

Time Taken

Student Worksheet – How fast?

Group Name_____   Group Members_____

Overview: To accurately be able to command the robot, you need to understand how fast it can go and what properties may change its performance. NASA have requested a detailed report, supported by data that you have gathered from your robot.

Make your robot drive forward for 5 rotations at 50% power

How long did it take to go 5 rotations?   _____ sec

What about 10% power?   _____ sec

70% power?   _____ sec

Fill in the time taken to complete 5 rotations on this table and plot your average on the graph

Power Level (%)	Run 1	Run 2	Run 3	Run 4	Run 5	Average
10						
20						
30						
40						
50						
60						
70						
80						
90						
100						

Draw a line of best fit through the data you have taken.

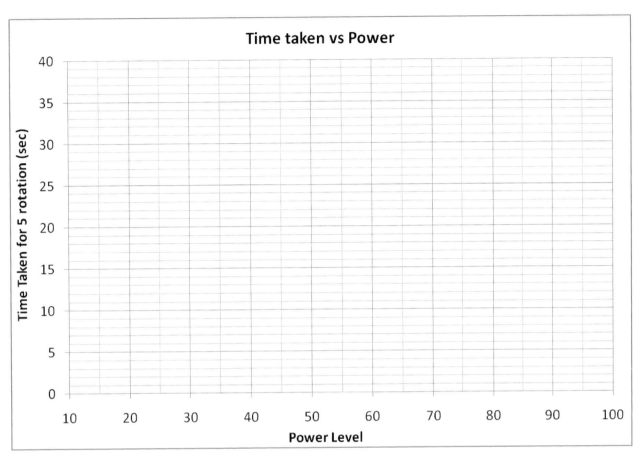

Based on this data, make a prediction as to how long it will take to
do 5 rotations at 65% power. _____ seconds

Mark your prediction on your graph in a different colour. Program your robot and see what happens.
How close were you?

Let us now convert this time taken into a speed.

How far does 5 rotations of the wheel take us? _____

Now convert each of these times and distances into a speed for each different power level. Fill in your
answers in the table below.

Power Level (%)	Time for 5 rotations	Speed (m/sec OR inches/sec)
10		
20		
30		
40		
50		
60		
70		
80		
90		
100		

Plot the speed of your robot against the power level on the following graph.

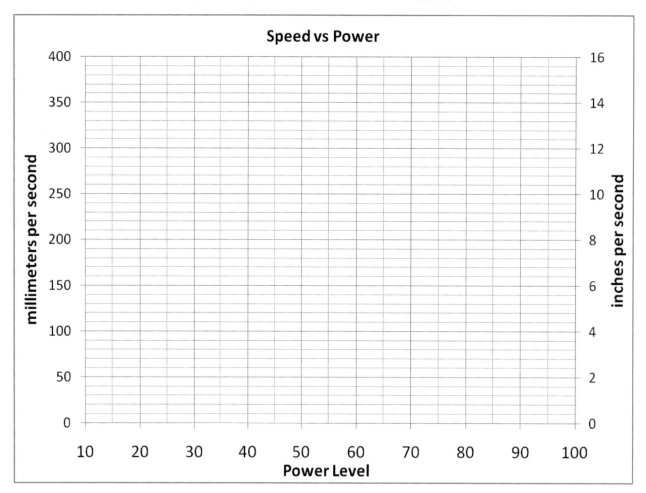

NASA have indicated that in some parts of NXTopia, the loose sand will make it difficult to drive quickly. They have calculated that the robot cannot exceed a maximum speed of 25 mm/s OR 10 inches/sec.

What power level is required to meet this speed? _____ % power level

Mark the speed on your graph in a different colour. Program your robot to travel for 10 seconds and check to make sure your robot stays within the guidelines.

What would happen if we were to run the same experiment on carpet?

What was the most difficult part of this challenge? _____

How did you go about solving it? _____

Student worksheet – How Many Sides?

Group Name_____   Group Members_____

Overview: Once on NXTopia, your robot will be required to identify interesting aspects for later analysis. Your robot will be required to mark off an area such that a passing satellite can easily identify the item in question. Initially you will be required to draw a square, but will then move onto other shapes and designs.

Build the drawing attachment and fix it to your robot and program your robot drive in a square, with each side 500mm (20") in length.

How many sides does a square have?   _____

How many angles?   _____

How many degrees in each angle?   _____

Could you use the loop block to make the program simpler?

Fill in the following table for other common shape

Shape	Number of sides	Internal angle	External angle	Turn Angle required by the robot
Octagon				
Hexagon				
Triangle				

What was the most difficult part of this challenge? _____

How did you go about solving it? _____

Student Worksheet – Help! I'm Stuck

Group Name_____   Group Members_____

Overview: Whilst on NXTpoia, your robot will undoubtedly come up against some terrains that are too difficult for the robot to navigate. NASA is worried about a particular chasm near the drop zone where the robot could conceivably get trapped. They have asked that you demonstrate your robots ability to detect such an obstacle and navigate out of the chasm.

Build a bumper to be attached to the front of your robot.

 There are several progressive steps we would like to make in order to solve this problem. Each program should be done individually and demonstrated to a teacher before moving on.

We would like our robot to drive forward until it encounters an obstacle.

- Drive until object is detected, then stop.
- Shout 'ouch!' when you hit an object
- Turn around when you hit the object.
- Repeat this action until you find your way out of the chasm

What was the most difficult part of this challenge? _____

How did you go about solving it? _____

Student Worksheet – Help! I'm (still) Stuck

Group Name_____   Group Members_____

Overview: NASA are happy with your bumper, but are concerned that the physical impact with the chasm walls will dislodge rocks sitting above. Modify your robot to include the Ultrasonic Sensor and run the same program, but this time recognising the walls before you touch them.

Connect the Ultrasonic Sensor to your robot.

Use the 'View' menu on your robot to see what types of readings you get with the Distance Sensor

View → Ultrasonic (cm OR inch) → Port 4

There are several progressive steps we would like to make in order to solve this problem. Each program should be done individually and demonstrated to a teacher before moving on.

We would like our robot to drive forward until it encounters an obstacle.

- Drive until object is detected, then stop.
- Shout 'hello!' when you are close to an object
- Turn around when you are close to the object.
- Repeat this action until you find your way out of the chasm

What was the most difficult part of this challenge? _____

How did you go about solving it? _____

Student Worksheet – Stay Away from the Edge

Group Name_____   Group Members_____

Overview: Another challenge the robot might face is safe navigation along a ridge line. Get too close and over you go. NASA has asked that you prove your robot is capable of staying away from the edge of a cliff.

Build a light sensor attachment for your robot.

We will need to take some readings to determine what values your robot reads for the table and the edge of the table.

View → reflected light → Port 3

What value do you get when your robot is on the desk?   _____

What value do you get when the light sensor is over the edge of the desk?
(hint: keep your hands and legs out of the way)   _____

What is your threshold number?   _____

There are several progressive steps we would like to make in order to solve this problem. Each program should be done individually and demonstrated to your teacher before moving on.

We would like our robot to drive forward until it recognises the edge of the desk. Get ready to catch it just in case!

- Drive until the edge is detected then stop.
- Shout 'whoops!' when you get to the edge.
- Turn around when you reach the edge.
- Repeat this action staying away from the edge of the chasm

What was the most difficult part of this challenge? _____

How did you go about solving it? _____

Student Worksheet – Did you Hear That?

Group Name_____   Group Members_____

Overview: The possibility of alien life forms present on NXTopia is quite high. NASA are concerned that they might be hiding and that the robot will not see them unless it can hear them approaching. Build a robot that can react to loud sounds.

We will need to take some readings to determine what values your robot reads for different noises.

View → Sound dB → Port 2

How loud is a clap?   _____

How loud is silence?   _____

Like previous challenges, we will be breaking this one down into small manageable programs

- Drive forward until you hear a sound and then stop
- Once the sound is heard, stop for 2 seconds and slowly turn around for 360 degrees of the robot.

How much duration does the wheel require to enable your robot to turn around 360 degrees? _____

We will now use 2 sensors to locate our alien.

- Drive forward until you hear a loud sound.
- Turn around slowly until you see an object within 30 cm (12")
- When you see your alien, stop and say hello

What was the most difficult part of this challenge? _____

How did you go about solving it? _____

Student Worksheet - MiniGolf Score Sheet

Group Name	Points					Total
	Round 1 Position A	Round 2 Position A	Round 3 Position B	Round 4 Position C	Round 5 Position D	

Student Worksheet – Dancing Robots

Group Name_____   Group Members_____

Artist:		Song Name:	
Section	Time	Description	Intended robot movement

Student Worksheet – As seen on TV!

Overview: NASA decided on using your design to fly to NXTopia. As a result of the associated publicity, many other people want to buy their own version of the robot. Come up with a marketing promotion to sell your robot.

Your presentation may consist of one or more of the following media formats as notated by your teacher

- School Newspaper article
- Video commercial
- PowerPoint Presentation
- Poster presentation
- Website
- Oral Presentation

Be sure to include the following information in your presentation

How does it look?

What can it do?

How does it move?

How does it sense its surrounding environment?

What are the standard missions it can perform?

Look back over your previous activities to help you answer these questions.

Remember, you are now pitching your idea to everyday people, not NASA scientists.

Chapter 20:

Building Instructions

These set of construction notes can be used to build the following assemblies

Base Design

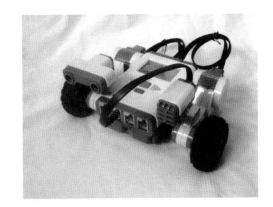

Touch Sensor Attachment

Light Sensor Attachment

Pen Attachment

Left Wheel Assembly - Base Design

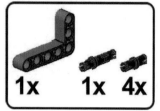

1x   1x 4x

1x

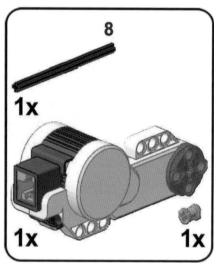

8

1x

1x   1x

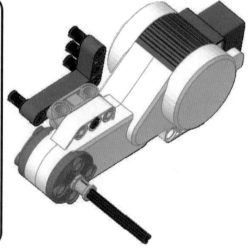

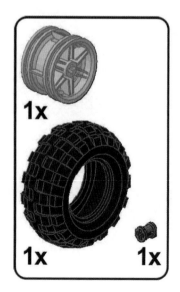

1x

1x   1x

Right Wheel Assembly - Base Design

4x

1x   1x

1x

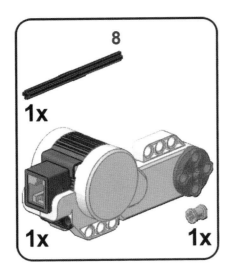

8

1x

1x   1x

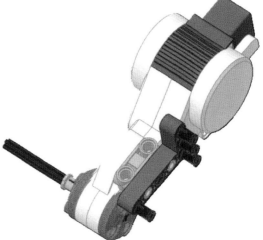

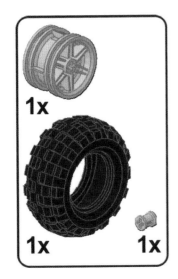

1x

1x   1x

Attach LEFT and RIGHT wheel assemblies to the NXT brick

Back Castor - Base Design

1

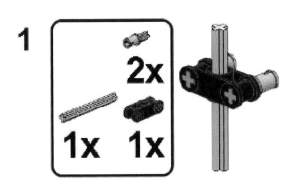

2x
1x 1x

2

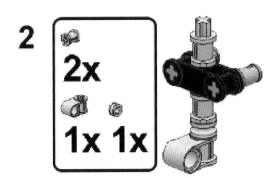

2x
1x 1x

3

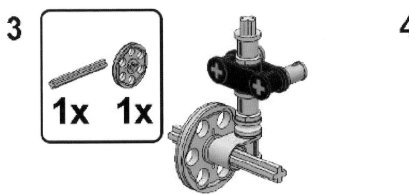

1x 1x

4

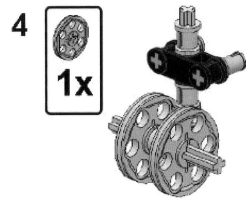

1x

5

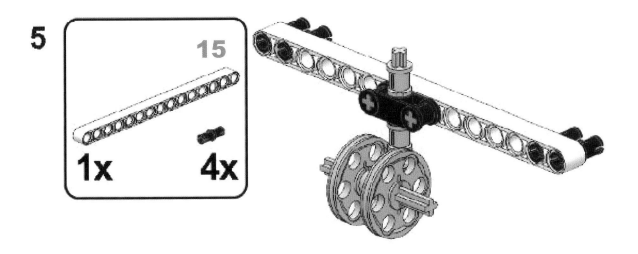

15
1x 4x

Turn the DomaBot around and attach the back castor bracket to the back of the motors

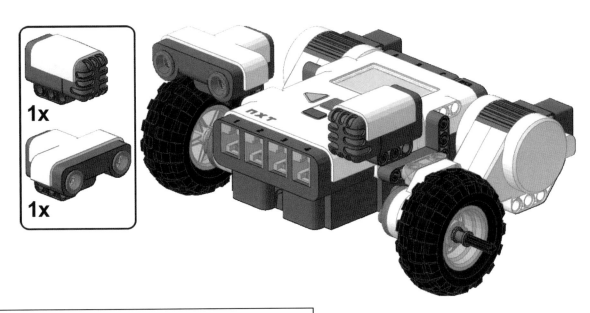

Connect the motor cables to 'B' and 'C' ports as shown

Building Instructions – Pen Attachment

Attach marker pen firmly with rubber bands

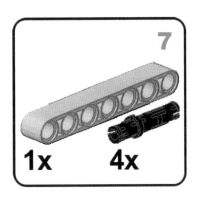

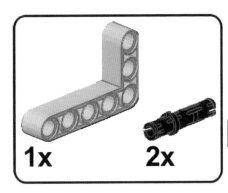

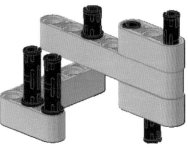

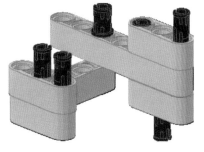

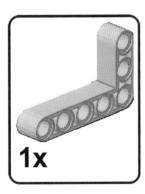

4x

2x

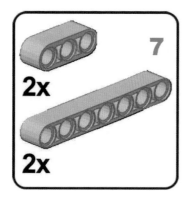

2x

7

2x

1x

1x

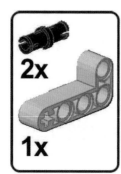

2x

1x

Building Instructions
Touch Sensor Attachment (Port 1)

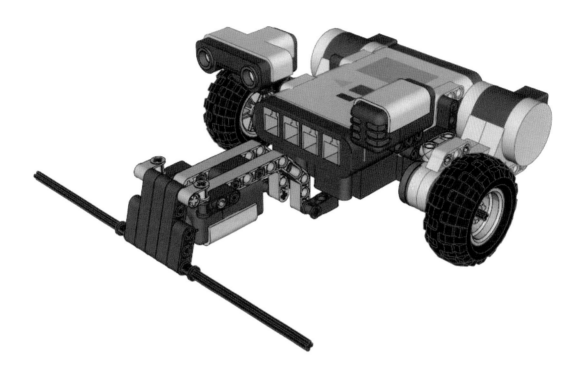

Connect Sensor cable to Port 1

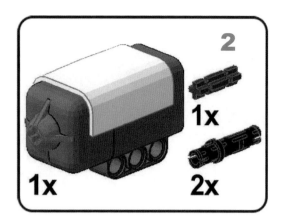

2

1x

2x

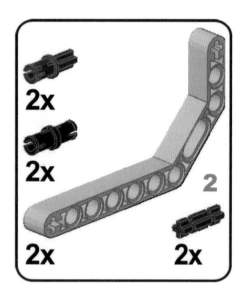

2x

2x

2

2x 2x

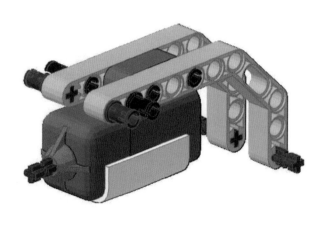

4x

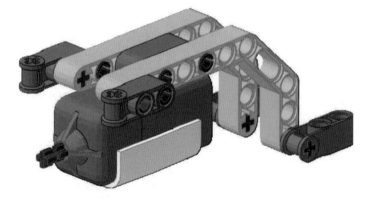

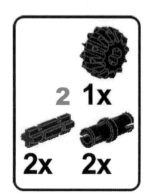

2 1x

2x 2x

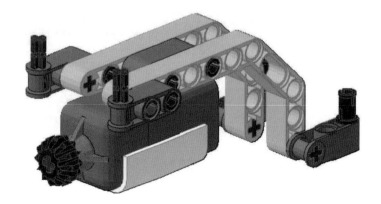

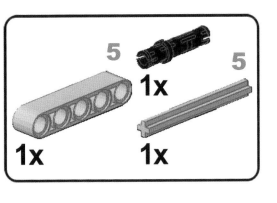

5

1x

5

1x **1x**

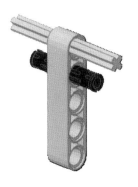

4x

5

2x

2x

2x

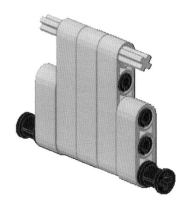

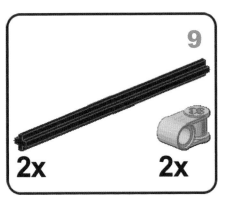

9

2x **2x**

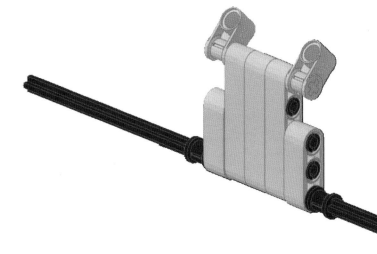

Assemble the 2 sections together and attach to the front of the DomaBot

Building Instructions 4
Light Sensor Attachment (Port 3)

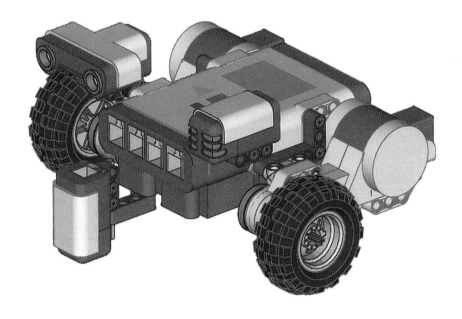

Connect Sensor cable to Port 3

1

2x

4

1x

1x

2

1x   2x

3

2x

4

1x

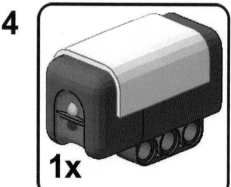
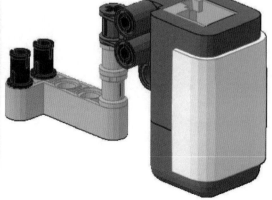